Face to Face with God in Your Church

ESTABLISHING A PRAYER MINISTRY

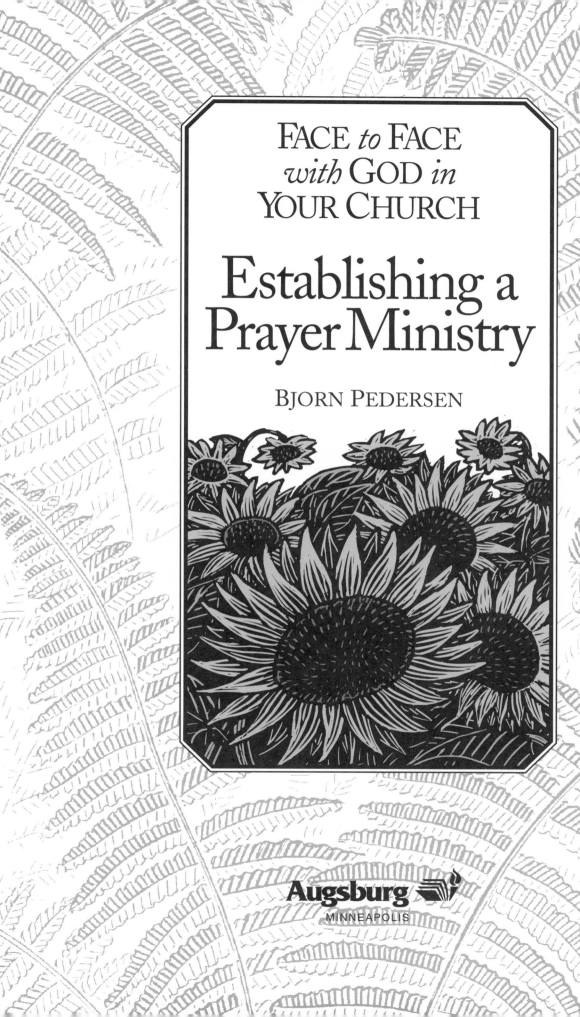

Face to Face
with God in
Your Church

Establishing a
Prayer Ministry

Bjorn Pedersen

Augsburg
MINNEAPOLIS

Face to Face with God

Face to Face with God in Your Church: Establishing a Prayer Ministry

Cover and inside design: Steven Broin, Visual Image Studio Inc.

Pedersen, Bjorn, 1944-
    Face to face with God in your church: establishing a prayer ministry / Bjorn Pedersen.
       p.   cm.
    Includes bibliographical references.
    ISBN 0-8066-2766-2 (pbk.)
    1. Prayer—Christianity. 2. Pastoral theology. 3. Prayer Groups—Christianity.
    4. Prayer meetings.   I. Title.
BV4013. P43 1995
248.3'2—dc20   95-2308
                                                       CIP

The paper used in this publication meets the minimum requirements of American National Standards for Information Sciences—Permanence of Paper for Printed Library Materials, ANSI Z329.48-1984. ∞™

Manufactured in the U.S.A.   AF 10-27662

99   98   97   96   3   4   5   6   7   8   9   10

To my mother,

who taught me to pray

when I was a little boy:

This book is dedicated to you

— Olga Pedersen —

with deepest appreciation

and

prayerful devotion.

CONTENTS

About the Cover

The fern is a symbol of piety because ferns grow deep in the forest, not by the highway, so they have to be sought out to be seen. The sunflowers, some with heads bowed and some upturned, remind us that when we come before God in prayer, we each come in our own way and with our own gifts.

About the Theme

The phrase face to face with God, *which identifies all the materials in this prayer ministry collection, was shaped by two Bible passages about relationships with God. In the Old Testament we read, "Thus the Lord used to speak to Moses face to face, as one speaks to a friend" (Exodus 33:11), and the apostle Paul wrote, "For now we see in a mirror, dimly, but then we will see face to face" (1 Corinthians 13:12).*

ACKNOWLEDGMENTS

Many thanks go to several people who made this project possible:

A special thanks to my wife, Phyllis, who patiently worked through each sentence and made many valuable suggestions.

Thanks so much to Beth Gaede at Augsburg Fortress, whose input I greatly appreciated and who made the manuscript better.

For the prayers and patience of my family and prayer ministry staff during the months of writing and rewriting, I'm deeply thankful.

Last, but certainly not least, I'm thankful to God for calling me into a ministry of prayer. May this book bring glory and honor to you!

INTRODUCTION

Prayer is perhaps the most universal expression of our faith. It is a practice in which all Christians participate more or less regularly.

Prayer takes many forms and expressions, depending on the prayer's theology, traditions, setting, and other factors. Some kneel while praying, others fall prostrate, some stand, and many prefer to sit comfortably. Some prayers are silent, others are spoken. Chanting, meditating, singing, crying, and shouting are but a few ways prayers are expressed.

Prayer has been part of human history since the beginning. Communication with God occurs in the first chapter of Genesis, at the dawn of creation. The earliest cultures showed an interest in "higher powers" and sought ways to communicate with them.

Throughout history, God has mobilized individuals to pray when important events were imminent. At the time of the Reformation, there was a renewed involvement in prayer. Reportedly, Martin Luther, himself a man of prayer, regularly spent three to four hours each day praying. In fact, according to the Apology of the Augsburg Confession, Luther seriously considered making prayer a third sacrament.

Ultimately, if we should list as sacraments all the things that have God's command and a promise added to them, then why not prayer, which can most truly be called a sacrament? It has both the command of God and many promises. If it were placed among the sacraments and thus given, so to speak, a more exalted position, this would move men to pray. [1]

The Methodist movement in England was also born of prayer. John and Charles Wesley spent much time praying and meditating.

Today there is a renewed interest in prayer, not only in America but in many parts of the world. For example, South Korea has seen a significant prayer movement. Prayer Mountain, north of Seoul, is an international center of prayer visited by people from many countries.

In 1992, *Newsweek* reported on the popularity of prayer.

Astonishingly, the current edition of Books in Print *lists nearly 2,000 titles on prayer, meditation, and techniques for spiritual growth—more than three times the number devoted to sexual intimacy and how to achieve it. "After the Bible,"* says Werner Mark Linz, president of Crossroad, a major publisher of serious religious books, "books on prayer are our biggest sellers." [2]

In its March 1994 issue, *Life* ran a lead article entitled "Why We Pray." [3] According to a telephone poll on prayer conducted by The Gallup Organization for *Life* in December 1993, 85 percent of the people surveyed reported that they pray. To the question, "How often do you pray?" 51 percent responded "once or twice a day" and an incredible 24 percent said "three or more times a day."

The content of respondents' prayers varied greatly, but 98 percent said they had prayed for their families and 92 percent reported praying for forgiveness. Twenty-three percent said they had prayed for victory in a sports event.

Of the people surveyed, 28 percent said they prayed for one hour or more. The largest number of participants (47 percent) indicated they prayed five minutes or less. To the important question,

"Have your prayers ever been answered?" 95 percent said yes.

At Community Church of Joy we began a prayer ministry, dedicated to encouraging prayer and spiritual development, in the fall of 1989. The church leaders felt a strong need to become more intentional about prayer, giving prayer a more important role in the church. We started by encouraging members of the church to spend time alone and together in prayer. Over the last six years, the prayer ministry has expanded significantly to encompass prayer activities ranging from prayer chains to an international conference on prayer, from community prayer involvement such as concerts of prayer to a prayer journey to Vietnam.

In recent years, the ministry has frequently been called upon to assist pastors, church leaders, prayer leaders, and others to help organize prayer ministries in other churches. The requests at times have been so heavy that we have been unable to respond to all the needs. That is one reason this handbook has been prepared, to encourage as many churches and church leaders as possible to develop prayer ministries.

The handbook is intended to be practical, easy to read and apply. The focus is on how to start an intentional program of prayer in your church. We provide many suggestions to get you started. While we think most of the ideas can be used in almost any church, we hope that you will freely adapt our suggestions to fit your church's size, setting, gifts, and needs. And we hope that you will respond to the leading of God's Spirit into new prayer ministries that will enrich your members and every aspect of your church's work.

Chapter One

WHY HAVE *a* PRAYER MINISTRY *in* YOUR CHURCH?

A few years ago I talked to a church leader when his denomination was in the process of launching a new plan of church growth and nurture. After we reviewed the plan, it occurred to me that nothing specific was said about prayer. I asked why. The answer was typical of what I hear when talking to church leaders: "Prayer is implied in everything we do."

Saying "Prayer is implied in everything we do" can be problematic.

Such an answer is both understandable and problematic. It is understandable because prayer ought to be involved in almost everything we do in church. Through prayer we ask to experience and express God's grace more fully, and we ask for God's protection. Prayer provides guidance for our decisions and power for service and ministry.

The church leader's answer is also problematic, because "implied" suggests prayer is expected simply to happen. It is not the focus, not a priority. At times, then, prayer is crowded out by other, seemingly more pressing activities. The result is well described in the hymn "What a Friend We Have in Jesus": "Oh, what peace we often forfeit; Oh, what needless pain we bear—All because we do not carry everything to God in prayer."

Before we begin to describe ways to develop prayer ministries, we need to stop and ask this crucial question: Why have a prayer ministry in your church?

Scripture Emphasizes Prayer

One traditional definition of prayer says it is "conversation with God." When we think about our relationship with friends and family, it becomes quickly obvious that spending time together, particularly time together in conversation, is one of the key ingredients to strengthening our relationships. God calls us to prayer to invite us into that closer relationship with him. No doubt that is why the Bible is full of examples of the importance of prayer. In fact, one excellent way to describe the Bible is to call it a book of prayers. It has been estimated that the Bible contains 667 prayers!

Scripture seems to assume that God's people pray.

Certainly, Jesus' example is very clear: he was a man of prayer. He prayed alone and with others. Furthermore, he encouraged those around him to pray. In Luke 11, Jesus teaches his disciples to pray. From the same passage (v. 1), we learn that John the Baptist prayed and taught his disciples to pray. In Matthew 6:5, we learn that Jesus assumes God's people pray: "And whenever you pray … ." Prayer is a key ingredient in our relationship to Christ.

The apostle Paul further underscores the importance of prayer in his first letter to Timothy. "First of all, then, I urge that supplications, prayers, intercessions, and thanksgiving be made for everyone … . This is right and acceptable in the sight of God our Savior" (1 Timothy 2:1, 3). As Timothy starts his ministry, Paul wants to make sure his young friend begins with a solid foundation—prayer.

In the familiar story of Jesus cleansing the temple in Matthew 21, Jesus quotes the prophet Isaiah (56:7) as he explains the true purpose of God's house: "My house shall be called a house of prayer" (v. 21:13). Scripture repeatedly emphasizes the importance of prayer, not only as an implied activity but as a highest priority.

We Need a Solid Foundation

Scripture describes prayer as a solid foundation for God's people.

When building any structure, the foundation is the most important part. Without a solid foundation, problems will occur sooner or later.

Jesus emphasizes this point in the parable of the two foundations in Luke 6:46-49 (or Matthew 7:24-27). One builder constructed his house on sand. When the storm came the foundation proved insufficient, and the structure came down. The other builder chose to place his house on a different foundation: a rock. His selection was well rewarded when the storm hit. His structure survived.

God is our solid foundation, and prayer is one way we nurture our relationship with God. Through prayer we learn to rely on God. In times of trials and storms, God has proven reliable. The witness of Scripture and of God's people through the centuries is that God will be with us during every storm. Through prayer we learn for ourselves the many ways our God is a God of compassion and power. Every church wants to lead people into prayer to enjoy to the fullest the relationship that undergirds and supports our life and ministry—as individuals and as a church.

Prayer Is a Resource

Prayer is a valuable resource for the church.

Except for God's grace, prayer is the most abundant—and underused—resource available to the church. Where prayer has been emphasized, the church has grown. God's love and generosity is evidence that God wants to be in relationship with us. So generous is God, in fact, that God is even more eager to give than we are to ask and receive. Scripture abounds with promises about prayer. For example, in Matthew 7:7-8, Jesus gives to the church one of the most powerful promises:

> *Ask, and it will be given you; search, and you will find; knock, and the door will be opened for you. For everyone who asks receives, and everyone who searches finds, and for everyone who knocks, the door will be opened.*

Prayer is a resource available to the church at all times. A prayer ministry will make use of this resource and provide strength, guidance, and blessings to the church staff and members, and beyond into the community and around the world.

A Story about Prayer

Whenever I begin to doubt the importance of prayer, I turn to the great story in Exodus 17:8-16 about Moses and Joshua fighting Amalek and his men at Rephidim. This narrative teaches us some important things about the relationship between prayer and ministry. When attacked, Joshua goes to the battlefield with some of the best soldiers. Moses, taking Aaron and Hur, goes to the top of a hill overlooking the battlefield. As Joshua enters the fray, Moses raises his hands toward heaven and prays.

As the day wears on, Moses gets tired and lowers his arms. A curious thing happens. Joshua was winning the battle as long as Moses was praying, but when Moses rests and quits praying, Joshua and his troops begin to lose!

The three men on the hilltop soon realize that Moses' hands must be lifted in prayer until the battle is won. They take a large stone and place it under Moses so he can sit comfortably. Then Aaron and Hur each hold up one of Moses' arms until the battle is over.

God, of course, could have used many avenues to win this battle. But two equally important battles were fought that day. Joshua needed to fight the battle on the front line. And Moses, Aaron, and Hur needed to wage the behind-the-scenes battle. Joshua needed Moses, and Moses needed Joshua.

One reason this particular story is recorded in Exodus is to show us the all-important connection between ministry and prayer. Ministries fail because churches and their leaders have not taken seriously the importance of prayer. Sometimes we are so busy with our work, we simply forget we need a team of people behind the scenes, standing by us and holding us up when we grow weary.

It is especially the people on the front line who tend to overlook the importance of prayer. But notice that Moses did not pray alone. He had two prayer partners who supported him. Even for a man of God like Moses, such support and encouragement were invaluable. If it was important to Moses, it is equally important for us today.

At times we might be tempted to think prayer is the easy way out. Not so. Prayer is hard work. Prayer took so much out of Moses he had to stop and rest. Have you tried to pray fervently for a couple of hours? Try it some time. You'll find it is much harder than you think. Moses prayed all day. He needed others to sustain him. There is an important lesson here: we need to make sure we surround ourselves with prayer partners who can sustain us!

The story of Moses praying while Joshua and his men fought the Amalekites provides a vivid reminder of the importance of prayer.

Prayer Works!

We just worked through one biblical account about the effectiveness of prayer. We don't have to look too far to see that the Bible and human history are full of examples of how God has answered prayers through the generations:

- Abraham prayed and persuaded God to have mercy on Sodom if there were ten righteous people in the town.
- Elijah prayed and called down fire from heaven.
- Daniel prayed and was saved from the lions.
- Paul prayed and the prison walls were shaken.
- Martin Luther prayed and the gates of Rome shook.
- John Knox prayed and Queen Mary trembled.
- John Wesley prayed and a great revival began in England.

When people pray, things happen!

There are several models for organizing prayer ministries.

We can count on God to answer prayers. When churches, pastors, church leaders, and members become more involved in prayer, we can expect their prayer to have an impact on people's relationships with God, with each other, and with God's creation.

Why Have a Separate Prayer Ministry?

Most prayer "ministries" fall into one of the following three models or patterns:

- The church is built upon prayer, and the central focus is prayer.
- Prayer is not organized into a separate ministry but is emphasized in certain areas of church life and practice (for example, in preaching and teaching).
- The prayer ministry is a separate ministry within the church.

All three models can work well in the right setting. You need to determine what works best in your church. An important consideration is what you feel God has called you to do in your church. There might be other models that would work better for you, or you might want to use a combination. Regardless of which model you follow, however, or even if you don't follow any specific model, prayer needs to be an important part of the life and ministry of your church.

Organizing a church around prayer is valuable—and difficult.

Relatively few churches use the first model. Such a church is organized around individual and group prayer. There is a real strength in developing a church around prayer, if that is your call from God. Prayer is a strong foundation and will nurture church members' relationships with God. However, a church that follows this model must constantly be aware of a subtle tendency to become introverted, focused only on development of personal piety. Churches might also note that this type of prayer ministry is extremely difficult to establish, simply because it is a major challenge to refocus an existing church, even if the new focus is on something as worthy as prayer. We can truly say it almost takes an act of God to move a church into this ministry. Obviously, this model is easiest to use when a church is new.

Churches that try to incorporate prayer in other ministries might think prayer is implied in all their work.

Churches following the second model tend to fall into one of two types: churches in which prayer is implied, and churches in which prayer is intentional. The challenges for churches in which prayer is implied have already been discussed: When prayer is implied, it is easy for prayer and prayer ministries to become lost in all the other programs of the church. The result can be that the church does not engage in prayer, or at least not in organized prayer, other than in a group setting (where individual prayer involvement and spontaneity can be lost). It takes a conscientious effort on the part of church leaders to encourage broad-based participation in prayer when prayer is viewed as an implied ministry.

Churches that incorporate prayer into all their ministries might also be intentional about the work of prayer.

Churches in which prayer is intentional have taken specific steps to ensure that prayer is incorporated into the life and ministry of the church. For example, the church develops training programs on prayer. Church activities include prayer time. Efforts are made to identify, develop, and call upon prayer gifts. In short, there has been a recognition of the importance of prayer and a conscious attempt to incorporate prayer on both the individual and church levels. The church might not have a separate prayer ministry, but prayer is an intentional focus.

There is still a danger that prayer programs can be swallowed up by other worthwhile programs in the church. With limited resources available, prayer could be pushed aside for more visible and established programs. However, this danger is significantly lessened when prayer is intentional, rather than implied.

The third model builds on the ideas discussed regarding intentional prayer. Resources are committed to establish a prayer ministry. This can be done on a volunteer basis, at least initially, depending on the size of the church. Typically, one prayer ministry, perhaps a prayer chain, a prayer small group, or a weekly prayer meeting open to the church, is organized and implemented. Other ministries are added as resources are made available.

Some ministries are difficult to introduce because we all tend to resist change. However, establishing a separate prayer ministry requires minimal change to existing programs and ministries. Simply begin a ministry of prayer, and you are on your way. (Creating a prayer ministry does require resources. However, it is possible to establish a ministry without hiring additional staff.)

Some of the important reasons for choosing to begin a separate prayer ministry are:

- A separate prayer ministry gives a clear signal to the church of the importance of prayer. It shows that the church is intentional about prayer.
- A separate prayer ministry does not easily get lost among the other programs of the church.
- A prayer ministry can foster development of a variety of prayer programs within the church.
- Prayer ministries are more likely to be developed and members are more likely to become involved in prayer ministries when someone is personally responsible for them.

The next chapter will help you discern whether God is calling your church to establish a separate prayer ministry at this time. It will also help you begin thinking about what such a ministry might look like.

There are real advantages to establishing prayer ministry as a separate ministry of the church.

Chapter Two

GETTING STARTED

We might be tempted, if we are interested in establishing a prayer ministry in our church, to start out by setting up a study group or a prayer chain or a team of callers to visit hospitalized and homebound members. But there is perhaps no ministry that requires a more carefully laid foundation than prayer ministry. Prayer ministry grows out of the heart of our relationship with God. So we need to begin there.

Pray Persistently

It should come as no surprise that the first step in starting a prayer ministry is prayer. We pray for God's wisdom and direction, for God to give us a vision for the prayer ministry. What is it that God wants to do here? What form should the ministry take? What resources are available? Is the church ready for a prayer ministry?

Believe it or not, perhaps the most common mistake made when planning a prayer ministry is failing to start with prayer. It seems so obvious that prayer comes first. But in our enthusiasm to start, we sometimes overlook prayer. We have a tendency to jump into things before we have prayed about them, and we sometimes see prayer as a superfluous activity.

God is more eager to give us direction and guidance than we are to ask. Many times in Scripture, God encourages us to ask. In the last chapter we looked at Matthew 7:7-8:

> *Ask, and it will be given you; search, and you will find; knock, and the door will be opened for you. For everyone who asks receives, and everyone who searches finds, and for everyone who knocks, the door will be opened.*

The verbs *ask*, *search*, and *knock* are in what is called the continuous present form. A better translation might be "ask, and keep on asking," "search, and keep on searching," "knock, and keep on knocking." What this translation makes clearer is that God invites us to persevere in asking for assistance.

This principle of persevering is emphasized in the parable of the persistent widow in Luke 18:1-8. We read in verse 1: "Then Jesus told [the disciples] a parable about their need to pray always and not to lose heart." It is so easy to stop asking. Our lives are complex and we often leave little or no time for

Churches that want to start a prayer ministry need to begin with prayer.

God is eager for us to ask for help.

God wants us to ask—and to keep asking.

The more time we spend in prayer at the beginning, the stronger the prayer ministry will be.

prayer. It is important, therefore, to encourage each other to continue asking God for wisdom and direction.

Churches getting ready to establish a prayer ministry might find that they need to pray for as long as two years—maybe even longer—before they are clear about what the ministry will be. But time spent first in prayer is time wisely spent. Prayer allows God to prepare our hearts, the hearts of all those who will be part of the prayer ministry, and the hearts and lives of those we will be praying for. The more time we spend in prayer preparation, the more effective our prayer ministry will be. It is as simple as that.

Pray about God's Will

We need to pray for God's guidance.

First, we need to ask for God's will to be revealed and for the Holy Spirit's guidance. What is it God wants to do in this church when it comes to prayer? God has specifically promised to grant us wisdom and direction when we ask. In James 1:5 we read, "If any of you is lacking in wisdom, ask God, who gives to all generously and ungrudgingly, and it will be given you."

How do we know something is God's will?

How do we know we have discerned God's will and that God has really answered "yes" to our prayers? We can ask God to confirm our sense of God's intentions, and God will show us the way, using any variety of ways to confirm plans. It can take some time before God's confirmations are in place, but they are worth waiting for.

The confirmation of other people helps us know we are following God's will.

Sometimes we will find confirmation through reading Scripture. Often confirmation comes through other people. Scripture talks about witnesses confirming what God has spoken. In Deuteronomy 17:6, we read that two or three witnesses were required to sentence a person to death. We are all familiar with Gideon and his fleece (Judges 6:35-40). And in 1 John 5:8, three witnesses attest to our salvation. Today God will still affirm decisions by various witnesses. If a number of people we trust agree that a particular prayer ministry should be established at a specific point, such confirmation helps us know with greater certainty what God is calling us to do and when.

Opposition from others does not necessarily mean an idea is not inspired. Listen to the opposition and determine why it surfaced. Many inspired ideas or visions have been opposed before they received approval. Opposition can help planners rethink and be clearer about what they think God is calling them to do.

Another source of confirmation is a sense of peace about a decision.

Another important source of confirmation is inner peace. God's inner peace is more than a feeling. It is a fruit of God's spirit. Philippians 4:7 describes it well: "And the peace of God, which surpasses all understanding, will guard your hearts and your minds in Christ Jesus." This special peace conveys God's approval. It is a peace that can come even when our outward circumstances are in turmoil. Relying on inner peace, however, can be kind of a tricky business, not because God's Spirit is untrustworthy but because we humans have a high capacity to fool ourselves into believing what we want to. Inner peace, therefore, should be seen as only one witness that should not be relied on without additional confirmation.

We can also receive confirmation through circumstances.

Circumstances can provide that additional indication of God's will. When things fall into place, resources for a prayer ministry are made available, people come forward to lead and participate—these things together, especially when accompanied by a sense of peace, can be affirmations of God's will. Each by itself is not sufficient, but together these signs point in the same direction.

Pray about God's Timing

We read in Ecclesiastes 3:1, "For everything there is a season, and a time for every matter under heaven." We need to pray for God to show us the right time to establish a prayer ministry. And that might mean we need to wait. Waiting is not easy, though. When we have made up our minds to do something, we want to get started. Waiting allows God to teach us patience, trust, and a greater ability to depend on him in all things. And waiting when we have a specific course of action in mind allows us to discern whether we are attending to God's plan or merely our own. Through the years, however, I have learned that the more patiently I wait, the clearer God's answer is. When I am impatient, I more often miss the answer.

Waiting on God's timing makes the job easier, once we determine that it is time to begin. We are busy and tend to rush into things without waiting for God's timing. In our impatience, we tend to run ahead of God. We forget that God might have a different timetable (not to mention a different agenda altogether). When we do that, we make much more work for ourselves than God intended. When we follow God's timing, everything seems to go more smoothly. God's energy and strength are in the project, not only our own.

Although we want to be sensitive in our efforts to discern God's will, God's grace is great. If we miss God's direction or timing, we can always start again. A mistake can be a learning experience that will help us make decisions in the future that are consistent with God's will. And God is gracious in granting new opportunities for us to start over and try again.

Praying for God's wisdom and direction is vital for our work, and we can count on God's leading. "For surely I know the plans I have for you, says the Lord, plans for your welfare and not for harm, to give you a future with hope" (Jeremiah 29:11).

Seek a Vision

A vision is a picture of how an organization will look, act, and minister at some point in the future. It is a conceptual plan with little detail that still addresses most areas that ministry will encompass.[4] A vision is a powerful energizer and motivator. A vision is a gift from God, allowing us to see through the eyes of God. Without a vision, it is hard to determine purpose, direction, and motivation. Ask, What is the ultimate goal for our prayer ministry? What is the prayer ministry's mission? What has God called us to do through prayer? Why do we need a prayer ministry? These and similar questions will help to begin defining the shape of the prayer ministry.

For a vision to have lasting impact, it needs to have three components.

Any vision, including the vision for a prayer ministry, needs to come from God. It has to be more than a human idea. It needs to be an inspired idea. We can count on God to give us a vision, because of God's unconditional love for all people. God's vision is a call from God to action. It is part of God's great commission to reach the world with the good news of God's grace in Jesus Christ. God will give us a vision, and God stands ready, willing, and able to back up the vision. In fact, there are times when we will have little else to stand on but

We need to pray for God's timing.

Waiting on God's timing makes the job easier.

A vision provides a sense of purpose, direction, and motivation for prayer ministry.

A lasting vision is not just a human idea.

the vision from God, God's call. Our prayer might become, "Lord, I have done everything I can. Now I stand on your promises, the vision, and your call. You will have to take it from here." But we can always trust that God's vision connects us to God and God's plans.

A vision can be expressed in different ways. For some it will come as a dream or an inspired idea that keeps coming back. Or it might come as a strong need we see clearly and feel we need to do something about. Sometimes a vision becomes stronger, even when we try to push it away. We can also expect God to confirm a vision in the same ways God confirms answers to prayers, as discussed above.

Many people, when they have seen a vision, feel inadequate to carry it out.

When we see the need and how great it is, we might very well feel inadequate to meet it. Many people in the Bible who received a vision from God and saw the task placed before them felt just this way. Look at Moses, Isaiah, and Jeremiah. They all made excuses—and they all took on the jobs anyway. The apostle Paul addresses this matter in 2 Corinthians 12 when discussing his vision and call. He is concerned about his inadequacies, his "thorn in the flesh." God assures him as God assures us today and every day: "My grace is sufficient for you, for power is made perfect in weakness" (v. 9).

Communicate the Vision

A lasting vision is clear and easily communicated.

The vision needs to be clear so it can easily be communicated to others. If leaders don't have a clear vision, it can't be meaningfully shared. Lack of clarity could be an indication that more preparation work is needed, or that the timing is not right. If the vision lacks clarity, leaders and church members can become confused and frustrated. For some, that is enough reason not to become involved.

Write down the vision. Seek to clarify ambiguous parts. If parts are missing, ask God again for wisdom and direction. Wait for answers. God will hear and answer our prayers because God wants us to pray. In fact, God is even more committed to our success in planning and implementing a prayer ministry than we are.

A lasting vision needs to be communicated to the group's members.

The vision needs to be lifted up for others to grasp and follow. One of the primary responsibilities of leaders is to articulate the group's vision for the members. A vision for prayer ministry is no different. It needs to be lifted up so others can see it, be reminded of it, and be propelled by it. And it isn't enough simply to share the vision once. We need to do it repeatedly. People are busy and tend to forget after a while what the vision was all about. We need to think about how the vision should be presented and when it would be best to share the vision again. A short, clear, catchy slogan can be a great help in communicating a vision. Even something as simple as "Prayer Works!" can be a vision builder, encouraging more people to become intentional about prayer.

There might be times when we feel frustrated and want to give up on the vision.

All three components are important. Even with God, though, it can still be difficult to get a vision implemented. We might burn out or become so frustrated that we want to give up. But in these low times, we return to the beginning: we pray. We pray for God to prepare the hearts of church leaders and members to see the vision and respond positively to the call of prayer. We pray for God's will to be done through us. We ask God to give clear direction. And we remember that seeking the heart of God and the guidance of the Holy

Spirit can take some time. We don't need to be in a hurry. After all, it is God's ministry and God will provide all we need. No matter how frustrated we feel, we can still have the peace of knowing the vision is God's idea and that God will support it. The vision is powerful and necessary for effective ministry. Don't proceed without it!

Explore Resources

The next step is to explore and obtain the applicable resources. What resources are available now that can assist us in starting a prayer ministry? Take an inventory. What books, literature, audiocassettes, or videotapes on prayer are in your church library? What helpful resources do church members have? Are there people in the church with gifts or interests in prayer?

Once the vision is in place, we can begin looking at our resources.

Once you have reviewed the available prayer resources, determine what is still needed. At this early stage, a church might look especially for these three resources:

- A book, such as this handbook on prayer ministry organization. (See For Further Reading on page 113 for other materials.)
- A resource person, not necessarily a member of your church, with some background and experience in prayer ministry and prayer ministry organization.
- At least one person who is willing to pray regularly for the planning, development, and implementation of the new prayer ministry. The faster this resource is identified the better. It is best, though not essential, if the person is a church member. (If no one is immediately available, call the director of intercession in the prayer ministry at Community Church of Joy [602/938-1460] and ask for prayer support. Someone will pray with you regularly.)

It might also be helpful to attend a conference or seminar on prayer, especially one that deals with organizing prayer ministry. Conferences provide an opportunity to talk to other church leaders who have more experience establishing a prayer ministry.

Chapter Three

PLANNING A PRAYER MINISTRY

nce the foundation of the prayer ministry has been laid—the church has prayed for God's wisdom and direction, developed and communicated a vision, and acquired some basic resources for guidance—it is time to develop a specific strategy, a blueprint for the ministry.

Planning Basics

Planning is important to ministry success. That seems self-evident, but many of us tend to act now and plan later. So begin by getting out your calendar and scheduling planning time for the coming year. Think about what you intend to accomplish at each point, how much time you will need, and who else needs to be involved. At first, you might want to schedule several longer sessions—half days or even full days—to work out big-picture concerns with key leaders. Later, you might need only a few hours once a month to fill in the details for a specific project, such as an upcoming class.

Schedule time for planning.

Remember that a plan is a tool, and a good ministry plan is dynamic, not static. Things change. A plan should be flexible enough to allow leaders and participants to respond to changing needs, circumstances, and opportunities. After it is drafted, approved, and implemented, it needs to be reviewed and revised regularly. Don't insist on following a plan no matter what the consequences. And don't let it sit on the shelf. Either course of action will soon render even the best plan useless.

A plan is a flexible tool.

A functional ministry plan grows out of the vision. The plan is a practical framework for putting into action the vision God has given the church. Keep asking, Does this adequately reflect the vision? Is this idea still within the original vision? If we include this activity, do we support the vision? Also ask, Are we being called to a new vision that requires a new course of action? Wrestling with these questions will help planners stay on course.

A good plan grows out of the vision.

Defining Values

One of the first steps in designing a prayer ministry is to pray for and decide what key values will be emphasized. What will have the most worth or be esteemed highly? What in the new ministry is nonnegotiable? The values emphasized will provide much of the shape of the basic vision.

Some values will be about the content or purpose of the ministry. A church might, for example, place a high value on asking God to lead and direct indi-

Decide on key values.

viduals and the church as a whole in their respective ministries. Emphasis might also be placed on asking God to inspire church members to pray.

Helping individuals to develop greater intimacy with Jesus is one possible value. Another value, in contrast, might be to support the growth of the whole church as a praying community. Or a church might try to do both. Generally, it is appropriate to start with individual growth and then foster expressions of prayer for outreach, but there are many examples of churches that decided to pray together about a concern, resulting in the growth of individuals' prayer lives.

Teaching people to pray and disseminating information about prayer might be highly esteemed, or a church might place more value on experiencing prayer. Or a church might seek to balance the two. Some churches are more geared to teaching, others to experience. This is an important choice, because it will determine whether a prayer ministry will focus primarily on teaching, training, and equipping pray-ers, or on providing opportunities for people to spend most or all their time praying, or on some of both.

A church might be most concerned about in-depth study and discipleship programs, versus a focus on reaching new pray-ers. With deep study comes maturity and confidence, the fruit of which is reaching out to others and inviting them to come and learn also, so this emphasis can address both concerns. Nevertheless, if the ministry's focus is limited to depth, it might be harder to attract people to the ministry, especially if they are new Christians.

There are a variety of possible values about the way the ministry will be carried out.

While some values are about the content and purpose of ministry, other values might be about the way the prayer ministry is carried out. Will the ministry emphasize, for example, a relational approach to interaction, in contrast to a task-oriented approach? Both approaches are necessary, but ministries tend to use one or the other. Which will be the focus of your ministry?

Of course, the values prayer ministry planners select need to be compatible with the overall vision of both the prayer ministry and the church. And the values need to respect that church's theology, setting, and traditions. Finally, whatever values are selected need to be clearly demonstrated in the ministry. Planners will want to make sure that they do not put forth one set of values on paper or in discussion, and support another in actual practice.

Developing a Strategy

Simply put, a strategy is a plan for getting things done. There are many ways to approach this phase of planning, which are discussed in detail below, but here are some things to keep in mind.

We need to ask God to show us what form the ministry needs to take.

Again, begin with prayer, since prayer is the foundation of the ministry. Pray about the vision for a prayer ministry, and look for the vision to take on a more definite shape. Look again at the values you think your ministry should emphasize. Ask God to show you the right type of prayer ministry and the place to begin. On the surface, this might seem obvious, but once we begin investigating, it is surprising how many options there are to consider. Do we start with an open prayer meeting in the sanctuary? Or would it be better to begin with a prayer Bible study in a member's home? Or do we start with a discussion group on Sunday morning as part of the adult education program? Maybe the pastor should begin with an off-site, weekend training program for leaders. Or do we begin with a prayer breakfast in a local restaurant? The choice of ministry and its location communicates something important to and about the church.

Be sure church leaders understand and approve of the prayer ministry. Better yet, make sure the ministry has enthusiastic leaders who will lead by example. If the church's leaders are not behind the ministry, continue to pray for God to prepare their hearts and minds.

Recognize that people have different backgrounds and levels of Christian maturity, as well as varying schedules and commitments. Design ministries that will be suitable for people at several levels of maturity and prayer experience, and that will accommodate a variety of schedules. A large church with a well-established prayer ministry, for example, might have a goal to offer open (corporate) prayer meetings every day of the week. Meeting times could vary from early morning to late afternoon. The focus of prayer could also vary, with one meeting focusing on healing prayer, another on prayers for the world, another on prayers for children.

Of course, such a model would probably be impossible to implement in smaller churches. But, using the same example, even small churches might provide two prayer meetings on different days and at different times, instead of just one weekly meeting. For example, one meeting could be held on Tuesday morning and another on Thursday evening.

Another possibility for a smaller church is to invite people who already participate in other church activities to make prayer a part of their time together. A regular fellowship group might begin with prayer for concerns related to families and schools in the community. A group that gets together to make quilts might take time before lunch to pray for the missions that will receive the quilts. Since one of the strengths of small churches is their strong sense of community, people in such settings might also respond well to a group that meets primarily for prayer but that also offers a chance to have some fun—an outing to the local high school's band concert or football game, a Sunday afternoon watching a video together, or time simply to enjoy refreshments and conversation after a time in prayer. With Spirit-inspired creativity, all kinds of worthwhile activities can be offered in conjunction with prayer time.

A Workable Ministry Plan

A useful, workable ministry plan includes the following elements:
- A compelling mission statement
- Practical goals
- Clear objectives
- Specific action plans
- Adequate job descriptions for key responsibilities
- A basic organizational chart showing who is responsible to whom
- A simple budget, if money will be spent

The rest of this chapter will elaborate on this basic outline.

The Mission Statement

The mission statement is a short statement of purpose and direction for the ministry. Drafting the mission statement is the single most important planning

> **It is important that church leaders understand and support the ministry.**

> **There are many creative ways small churches can offer a variety of prayer experiences.**

> **The mission statement is key.**

activity because the mission statement communicates the vision in one or two simple, clear sentences, and all the other basics flow from it.

Start by identifying the vision's key ideas. Express these in single words or simple phrases, and examine each one: Is this really descriptive of the vision? Can it be said better or more clearly? Can it be said in fewer words?

Try to state the mission in one clear sentence.

Try to write the entire mission statement in one clear sentence. For example:
- Our mission is to pray.
- Our mission is to pray for … .
- The mission of our ministry is to pray and to teach others to pray.
- Our mission, inspired by the Holy Spirit, is to pray and to provide prayer opportunities for our members.
- The mission of the prayer ministry is to pray, teach others to pray, provide prayer opportunities, and participate in the fulfillment of our church's vision and mission, as we are inspired by the Holy Spirit.

Then look at the strengths and weaknesses of your sentence.

All these mission statements are short, clear, and focused. The first, however, does not address some important functions of most prayer ministries, such as teaching prayer to others and developing specific prayer activities. The second statement directs the ministry's mission toward prayer for specific purposes, such as the church, community, or nation. The focus is sharp, but the scope is probably narrower than it needs to be.

The third statement is a good one for any prayer ministry, although it doesn't include any reference to Jesus or to Christianity, while the fourth statement refers to the Holy Spirit. The fifth statement has the advantage of specifically referring to the church's vision as the beginning of the prayer ministry's mission.

Goals

Goals provide more details about the mission plan.

Goals are broad statements of intended accomplishments. A goal describes the vision in greater detail than the mission plan. This process of becoming more specific continues through most of the ministry plan.

Only two or three goals are needed. One goal could come from each key word or idea in the mission statement. Members should be able to understand quickly how the two are related.

An example.

Let's look at an example. Assume the prayer ministry has the following mission statement: The mission of the prayer ministry is to pray, teach others to pray, and provide prayer opportunities for our church's members, inspired by the Holy Spirit. The mission statement identifies three major areas around which goals can easily be developed:
- Encourage people to pray and/or to pray more.
- Teach church members and others to pray.
- Develop opportunities for people to become more involved in prayer and prayer ministry.

Objectives

Objectives will further define the ministry.

Objectives are even more detailed than goals. They describe tasks to be accomplished and need to be specific, quantifiable, and time measured, as well as realistic and achievable. Objectives should also be challenging and help the church grow. If objectives are too ambitious, however, people might give up without reaching them. It takes some wisdom to establish objectives that provide a healthy challenge and are still achievable.

Let's look at the third goal above: Develop opportunities for people to become more involved in prayer and prayer ministry. What can be done to accomplish this?

- By March 1, research resources for prayer ministry.
- By April 1, attend a prayer conference.
- By June 1, identify two additional prayer opportunities that fit into the present prayer program.
- By September 15, introduce the two new prayer opportunities to the church.

These objectives provide specific steps which, if followed, likely will lead to the fulfillment of the goal.

To clearly define what will be accomplished within the prayer ministry, ask questions like, What do we hope to accomplish? How will the prayer ministry enhance the overall ministry of our church? Suppose one of a church's goals is: Encourage people to pray and/or to pray more. Objectives for that goal might include:

- Twice a year, offer a class during the adult forum on how to begin praying.
- Establish a small group of five to seven people that will meet twice a month for at least four months to help experienced pray-ers grow in their prayer life.
- Prepare a monthly newsletter column about prayer needs and answers.

These objectives identify a cluster of activities that will all contribute to the goal.

Objectives might also describe what needs to happen in order to reach all of the goals as a whole. For example, the first objective might be about drafting a ministry plan. This is an excellent starting point because the document produced can be presented to and discussed by leaders and members of the proposed new prayer ministry. Other typical objectives focus on organizational development, attendance expectations, and targets for training and equipping ministry leaders and participants.

Expect to have more objectives than goals, but remember that too many objectives can be difficult to monitor. The more complex the plan becomes, the more administration it needs and the greater the likelihood of frustration and inadequate follow-up. People are reluctant to take part in something they do not understand.

If they are going to be helpful, objectives need to be reviewed regularly. Some leaders do this monthly, others quarterly, semiannually, or annually. It makes sense to start with more frequent reviews in the beginning. After the plan seems to be well in place, the reviews can occur less often.

Action Plans

Each objective is accompanied by a number of action plans. An action plan is a specific step toward accomplishing the objective. When all the steps are completed, the objective should have been reached. The number of action plans may vary, depending on the complexity of the objective, but in general simplicity and clarity are very important for effective action plans.

Objectives might describe the steps needed to carry out a goal.

Objectives might describe a cluster of activities that contribute to a goal.

Objectives might describe concerns related to several goals.

Too many objectives can be difficult to monitor.

Objectives need to be reviewed regularly.

Action plans outline the specific steps needed to fulfill each objective.

An example.

How does an action plan work? Let's turn to an example from the previous section.

Mission statement: The mission of the prayer ministry is to pray, teach others to pray, and provide prayer opportunities for our church's members, inspired by the Holy Spirit.

Goal 3: Develop opportunities for people to become more involved in prayer and prayer ministry.

Objective 1: By March 1, research resources for prayer ministry.

Action plans:

- Check with the local library for books on prayer opportunities.
- Contact one or more Christian bookstores for books, audiocassettes, and videotapes on prayer opportunities.
- Read and review the selected materials.
- Contact someone who is involved in an established prayer ministry.

Job Descriptions

Job descriptions let people know what is expected of them.

There are three basic steps for developing job descriptions.

When a new ministry is started and people are invited to take a leadership role, they want to know what kind of commitment they are being asked to make. The best way to answer is to provide a job description. A job description might not be needed for every position, but at least the key leaders need one.

Follow these simple steps when developing job descriptions:

- Identify the key positions within the organization. It can be very helpful to sketch a tentative organizational chart first, so you can see the big picture. (See the next section.)
- Once each position has been identified, describe the responsibilities. The descriptions need to be short and easy to understand, yet long enough to be thorough. Generally, it is better to err on the side of brevity and simplicity.
- Job descriptions should be reviewed regularly to be sure they are accurate, since expectations and responsibilities can change with time. The person who fills the job should help with the review, since he or she is in the best position to know whether the description is working or not. This would be a good time to evaluate whether the job is contributing to the mission as originally envisioned.

Job descriptions might include two sets of expectations.

It might be helpful to divide job descriptions into two sections: specific ministry responsibilities applicable to this particular position, and general attributes and involvements expected of all church leaders.

The following elements might be included in a list of specific ministry responsibilities.

- Indicate the name of the ministry or activity the job description covers.
- Include the mission statement for the ministry or at least the purpose of the job.
- Describe the duties and responsibilities of the position.
- State for how long the person is expected to fill the position (for example, one year) and how much time per week or month the task is expected to take. Include a list of meetings the person is expected to lead or take part in.
- Indicate what the jobholder is expected to do to increase skills (for example, attend an annual conference on prayer).

- State to whom the person is responsible and what reporting mechanism will be used to track accomplishments, recommendations, and proposals requiring approval.
- State who is responsible to this person.

A general description of attributes and commitments expected of church leaders might look like this:

General expectations.

Leaders of ministries at _____ Church are expected to:

- Be a member of this church.
- Be committed to prayer and spiritual growth.
- Pray regularly for the church, its leaders, and its mission.
- Worship regularly.
- Make a financial commitment to the church and its mission.

It is common to have the people who accept the positions sign the job descriptions. Signing gives them a deeper sense of commitment to the ministry. It also communicates the importance of each position in fulfilling the church's mission. Accompany the signing with recognition and appreciation by the church and its leaders.

Ask people to sign their job descriptions.

Organizational Charts and Budgets

An organizational chart is a graphic, simple, easy-to-understand description of an organization's structure. Such charts can help leaders communicate the ministry vision to other leaders, as well as to current and potential ministry participants. They show how the ministry is organized, and who is responsible to whom. They will help keep the ministry growing in a direction consistent with the vision of the church. Because organizational charts do serve as a map for the future, even small churches, which require only a simple chart, should take the time to develop a chart as the ministry grows.

An organizational chart is a communication tool.

A chart can show the relationship among individual ministries within the church, as well as among individuals within a particular ministry. If names of people in various positions are available, they can be included, although sometimes including specific names draws attention to individuals rather than positions, and makes the chart go out of date more quickly. If the ministry has a significant turnover rate or if the chart is large, updating names can be inconvenient. If names are included, keep a generic chart, too.

There are several disadvantages to including the names of jobholders on the chart.

Many of the prayer ministries described in the appendixes require money—for study and training materials, office supplies, facility or transportation rental, and so forth. A budget should be developed for each ministry that needs and manages money. The budget indicates what money has been allocated to the ministry. (Of course, someone also should follow up and account for how these funds are used.) Bookstores and libraries have much information on budgets. In general, the best budget is as simple as possible. Church leaders and ministry participants should pray for the budget and the finances regularly.

If a ministry needs and manages money, a budget is needed.

Sharing the Ministry Plan

A ministry begins with a good foundation built through prayer and planning. The proposed plan is reviewed, evaluated, and possibly revised. Then it is time to share the plan with others.

Share the plan to seek suggestions for improvement and/or confirmation of the plan.

The purpose of sharing a ministry plan is twofold. First, seek input about how to improve the plan, or confirmation that the plan is an expression of God's vision for the church. During this phase of the process, be especially attentive to ideas that seem to recur in the discussions.

Two groups in the church ought to be consulted, unless they have already been involved: the church leadership group (it is assumed that the pastor and perhaps several others have been actively participating already) and the church's prayer community, if one can be identified. The wisdom and counsel of both groups are valuable and necessary for successful implementation of the plan.

Share the plan to seek endorsement.

The second purpose for sharing a ministry plan is to ask for endorsement. Pray for God's wisdom and timing and for God to prepare the hearts of the presenters and the listeners to receive and embrace the prayer ministry. A possible strategy for sharing the plan is as follows:

- Begin with people and groups who will give the greatest support. This will build both confidence and momentum.
- Next, or perhaps simultaneously, share the plan with the leaders of the church. If they are not behind the plan, it is almost impossible to win support for it from the church. If fact, if the leaders do not endorse the plan, do not present it to the church. Return to prayer, revise the plan, and/or try a different approach for winning support.
- Finally, when the leaders have given their support, present the plan to the rest of the church so everyone has a chance to learn about and support it.

There are three steps to presenting a plan.

The actual presentation of the prayer ministry plan could incorporate the following steps:

- First, of course, lay out your plan, beginning with the vision.
- Next, ask for the group's input and listen to what they have to say.
- Assuming no strong objections have surfaced, ask for the group's support of the vision of the ministry and the plan for implementing it.
- If objections to the plan have been raised, try to clarify what needs to happen before the plan can be adopted.
- Ask for group members' involvement in the new ministry.
- Finally, pray that all who are touched by this ministry will be receptive to it and ultimately transformed by it.

Chapter Four

AVOIDING PITFALLS

hen we begin to think about and implement a prayer ministry, we will most likely face a number of challenges. Challenges are not all bad. They often bring us to our knees in prayer. There are, however, some things we can do to avoid the worst pitfalls when we establish a prayer ministry.

Set an Example

It is difficult for a church to fully catch the vision of prayer unless the leaders are willing to set a good example. On occasion, a leader will ask me what is the most important thing he or she can do to develop a praying church. The expected and right answer is to pray for a praying church. In fact, I cannot emphasize too much how important it is for church leaders to pray and to provide an example others can follow. Throughout Scripture, we find many instances of the people of Israel following the example set by their leaders, for both good and ill. If the church leaders are committed to participating in and holding up prayer as a high priority, the church will follow.

The example of a church's leaders is key to starting a prayer ministry.

Church members who are not in positions of leadership but who have caught the vision of prayer and wish others shared that vision, might consider the following:

- Continue to pray that God will reveal to the church's leaders the importance of prayer.
- Ask others who share the vision for a prayer ministry to join in this prayer.
- Enthusiastically support and pray for whatever ministry God is doing in the church. Especially remember to pray for God's support and guidance for the leaders of the church's existing ministries.
- Wait patiently for God's timing. If it is God's plan for a church to have a prayer ministry, it will happen. I have yet to read in Scripture or hear about a church or a person who prayed too much. The Bible admonishes us to pray more, not less.

People who are not church leaders can act to bring about a vision for prayer ministry.

Start with the Basics

With all prayer, we need to begin with the basics, to crawl before we run. It is especially important for new prayer groups or for groups that expect to be welcoming to new pray-ers to lay a prayer foundation before becoming too specialized. The group probably will want to begin by reading about and dis-

The way to begin learning to pray is to pray.

cussing prayer. But groups should avoid spending all their time talking about prayer. To learn to pray, pray!

The tendency to talk about prayer rather than do it is one of the biggest challenges I have found in prayer, one we must be aware of and try to avoid. There is absolutely no alternative to prayer. It is like learning to swim. We can read about it. We can talk about it. We can study it. But until we get into the water and actually swim, our information doesn't mean much. Yes, we read about, talk about, and study prayer. But in the end, the most important part of prayer is the actual praying. So, even if the group is entirely made up of people who think they don't know how to pray, the group should always conclude its time together with some form of prayer.

There are many ways to pray.

Prayer is multifaceted. It includes both individual and group prayer. We can pray for the healing of spirit, soul, and body (see 1 Thessalonians 5:23). We can offer intercessory prayer for other people, churches, or countries. Through listening prayer, we learn to be sensitive to the Holy Spirit's guidance and direction. Some Christians do what is sometimes called warfare prayer, praying for the kingdom of light to defeat the kingdom of darkness (examine Ephesians 6:12).

There are a number of simple ways to teach beginners to pray.

Every kind of prayer, however, is at heart simply conversation with God. While beginning pray-ers probably already have a sense of that, they might want help learning to pray as part of a group. Three simple, effective, and non-threatening ways to begin praying in a group are:

- **Silent prayer.** Form a circle and hold hands. When one person has finished praying silently, that person gently squeezes the next person's hand, signaling him or her to begin praying silently. Or everybody can pray silently at the same time.
- **Sentence completion prayers.** The leader starts a sentence, which group members complete. For example, they might begin the prayer, "Dear Lord, because you love me, I can … ." Someone continues. This is a good way to make the potentially difficult transition from silent prayers to praying out loud.
- **Short sentence prayers.** To start, invite participants to write out their prayer sentences. Then ask them to read (pray out loud) their sentences. Next, invite the group to experiment with short, spontaneous prayers, ideally on an agreed upon topic.

Be patient, especially with new members. Avoid the temptation to push people into forms of prayer for which they do not feel ready. In fact, it might be a good idea to offer a prayer group specifically for new members. The primary goal of the group would be to introduce people to prayer in a nonthreatening way.

Keep It Short

Short prayers are often the most effective.

Resist the temptation to have lengthy prayer gatherings. Both prayers and meetings should be short and to the point. Lengthy get-togethers will only discourage newcomers and frustrate others.

There are times, of course, when long prayers are both necessary and desired; for example, during a twenty-four-hour prayer vigil, for special prayer concerns, or with a group of well-trained, experienced pray-ers who are used to spending significant amounts of time in prayer. However, when a group is starting out, brevity and focus are important. Encourage participants to say short prayers. If they want to pray more, they can offer more prayers. Longer prayers can come with more seasoning and experience.

I have to remind myself about short prayers occasionally, because it is so easy to get involved in lengthy ones. At times, we might feel that God is more likely to grant a request if we offer a long prayer. We might sometimes also pray for an audience, trying to impress people with our profound content or beautiful prayer style. We need to remind each other that Jesus looks to the heart, rather than to form, style, or presentation.

Use Everyday Words

Language choice is important in prayer groups, especially when we are working with people new to the church. The wrong language can make people feel insecure and unwelcome.

When we pray, we want to use everyday language.

It is perfectly all right to use current, everyday language. We can encourage people to talk and pray as they normally would. We do not need to use special terminology and language that says, "I'm more spiritual that you are." Especially when working with new prayers, emphasize being natural and being yourself. We will want to practice these guidelines ourselves, because the group has a tendency to follow the leader.

At the same time as we try to use everyday language, we can challenge each other to use meaningful language. For example, some groups might be fond of a word like *bless*. They might try to find other words and phrases that make them think again about what exactly is being requested. They might, for example, ask God to "favor," "delight," or "smile on" the person or situation being prayed for. Or rather than "giving God the glory," they might talk about "giving God the credit."

We also want to use language that is meaningful to us.

It is very easy to fall into churchy language. Ask God for wisdom and creativity in the use of language that is both authentic and welcoming, that will help people feel free to offer their own prayers.

Choose a Focus

"Choose a focus" is good advice for prayer ministries that involve groups of people gathering for prayer. Without a focus, such prayer groups tend to wander and gatherings can drag. People become frustrated and bored if there is little or no direction. And prayer groups that have no focus encourage people to pray a little bit about a lot of things, rather than to pray in depth for a few concerns. Therefore, whether a church is attempting to establish a new prayer ministry or has been involved in prayer activities for some time, helping prayer groups focus is important.

As in other groups, a prayer group needs a focus or purpose.

A general (as opposed to focused) prayer group simply agrees to meet at a particular time and place. There are advantages to having a general group. Such a group can be responsive to a wide variety of needs, and general groups tend to be welcoming to newcomers. Even if a church has only one general prayer group, though, it might be wise, for the reasons mentioned above, to choose a focus. At least ask for group members' personal prayer requests and/or use prayer requests from the church. Here are some things we have learned about focusing a prayer group.

A focus helps keep a prayer group motivated and organized.

A focus, such as a topic or a specific need, helps organize the group's prayer, while allowing the group to stay flexible enough to address special needs that arise during the sessions. A focus also helps attract people who might come simply because they share an area of concern.

For example, a group might meet on Wednesdays at noon to focus on praying for world evangelization, attracting people who are concerned about missions. A Thursday noon prayer group might focus on healing prayer, attracting people who are struggling with physical and spiritual health issues.

If a church has more than one prayer group, groups can be organized around demographics.

If a church has more than one prayer group, prayer can be organized around demographic groups. For example, on Monday mornings a prayer group for young mothers might meet. Provide nursery services so the women can leave their children with a responsible person while praying together. On Friday mornings, encourage seniors to take part in another open prayer meeting especially organized for them.

It seems to work well to group people by interests, age, and general station in life. Young parents like to talk about children and child rearing. Retired people with more time to spend might enjoy a brunch with their prayer meeting. However, even though prayer groups might target special populations, clearly convey that all prayer meetings are open to anyone.

Even groups that have a focus can benefit from selecting specific topics for prayer.

Prayer groups that have an identified focus can benefit from selecting even more specific topics for prayer times. For example, during the Wednesday world prayer meeting, the prayers might focus on a particular country and its special problems. The leader can come prepared with a prayer topic. Some churches establish weekly, monthly, or quarterly prayer topics. A group might also use prayer requests from the church to set a direction. For example, a group that meets for healing prayer might begin with individual prayer requests for healing and end by studying a particular aspect of healing.

Report Positive Results

Both those who pray and those who ask for prayers need to hear about how God answers their prayers.

One of the most difficult challenges in prayer ministry is to find creative ways to let pray-ers and others know how God answers their prayers. Letting people know how God has answered prayers, however, is important for many reasons.

- Reports about answers to prayer show us the grace and power of God at work in the world. They give us a sense that God is with us, right here and now, not just "way up there," removed from our needs and struggles.
- Part of our calling as Christians is to offer God thanks and praise. So telling others about God's answers to our prayers is as enjoyable to God as it is to us. When we tell someone about the good things God has done, we thank God for answering our prayers and celebrate God's kindness and generosity.
- Hearing about God's answers to prayers reminds us that God does not necessarily answer every prayer with a "yes." We are reminded, rather, of the many ways God shows love for us and that God is committed to comforting, nurturing, protecting, directing, and empowering us.
- Such stories are a great source of encouragement for all those who pray.
- Most people are interested in personal stories about how God's grace makes a difference.

People might tell about answered prayers during a worship service, perhaps at the point when people make requests to be offered during the prayer of the church. Other possibilities include setting aside a time to share at open prayer meetings, placing "Answers to Prayers" forms in the pew racks and reading them to the gathered worshipers from time to time, scheduling celebrations in which the focus is on how God has answered prayers, printing one or two stories about answered prayers every month in your church's newsletter, and so on.

A church might refer to this type of witness as a praise report, a faith story, an answered prayer story, a personal testimony, or any other term that is clear and makes it comfortable for people to talk about God's answers to prayer. Some members, of course, will feel uncomfortable with this at first. Give people time to warm up to the idea. Never push anyone to share a story. Some feel such stories are too personal. Some might think the person telling the story is bragging, others might believe the reports sensationalize the experiences. Don't give up. Given some time, people will look forward to hearing about the good things God is doing.

Chapter Five

PRAYER MINISTRIES

Prayer is exciting and offers many opportunities for ministry. In Appendixes A, B, and C on pages 43 through 102, prayer ministries are described and suggestions offered to help you plan and organize such activities in your church. Before you begin considering specific prayer ministries for your church, keep these points in mind:

- The various ministries described in this handbook are offered as a prayer smorgasbord. Select the ministry that suits your church best.
- If your church does not already have an intentional, broad prayer ministry, start with only one ministry. Don't overwhelm yourself or your church. Try to find one idea that can be successfully implemented in your church. Later, in God's time, add others as you think the church is ready. Starting cautiously will make life easier for you and the church.
- No matter what specific ministry you begin with or how your overall prayer ministry grows, design frequent opportunities for members and friends of your church to learn more about prayer. (See the back cover of this book for a list of other components of *Face to Face with God*. These resources would be excellent starting points for the education component of a prayer ministry, and each resource includes a list of other books and materials that can be used for further study.)
- The ministries described in this handbook range from annual events to daily activities. The required commitment level varies also. Start with an activity that is easy to organize, given your church's calling, gifts, and resources. Your church's first experience should be positive and exciting. The more complex the activity, the greater the challenge and the more likely people will feel discouraged, especially at the beginning.
- Review the description of the prayer ministry, knowing that the idea will probably need to be adapted to fit your situation. Every church is different, and circumstances vary from church to church. Make adjustments according to your needs. Use ideas that fit, and reject or modify parts that do not apply.
- Be open to ideas from other places. This list of prayer ministries is not meant to be exhaustive but to provide you with a wide range of alternatives, so both novices and those with experience will find workable, inspiring ideas.

Appendixes A, B, and C include descriptions of a variety of prayer ministries.

Choose the ministries that suit your church.

Help people grow.

Start with something easy.

Adapt ideas to fit your needs.

Look for ideas from other places.

Prayer Ministry Descriptions

The ministry descriptions all follow the same format.

The various prayer ministries outlined in this handbook are divided into three categories based on the ministry's complexity and frequency, although complexity is the more significant factor. A prayer ministry that is simple to organize but that occurs frequently, therefore, would likely be in the start-up category.

The three categories are called start-up, intermediate, and advanced ministries. The sheet on each prayer ministry includes the following information:

- Title
- Category
- Synopsis
- Resources Required
- Description

Here is a list of the ministries in each category.

Appendix A: Start-Up Ministries
- Staff Prayer
- Prayer Outreach
- Prayer Focus Card
- Prayer Calendar
- Prayer Lists for Special Needs
- General Prayer Chain
- Sanctuary Prayer Chain (with intermediate options)
- National Day of Prayer (with intermediate options)

Appendix B: Intermediate Ministries
- Prayer Coordinator
- Prayer Tape Ministry
- Prayer Vigil
- Prayer Retreat or Seminar
- Open Prayer Meeting
- Prayer Small Group
- Membership Intercession Ministry (with advanced options)
- Prayerwalking
- Prayer Breakfast (with advanced options)
- Prayer Emphasis Week or Month (with advanced options)
- Prayer Care Program
- Prayer Chapel

Appendix C: Advanced Ministries
- Prayer Team Ministry
- Ministry of Intercession
- Healing Prayer Ministry
- Prayer Partnership Ministry
- Intercessory Support Ministry
- Prayer Telephone Ministry
- Concert of Prayer
- School or College of Prayer
- House of Prayer

Chapter Six
REVIEWING *and* REVISING

After your prayer ministry has been in place for some time, it is important to review its progress and direction. With time, your original focus might have changed or even been lost.

There are no set guidelines or timetables for such reviews, but most of them occur quarterly, semiannually, or annually. In addition, as soon as you suspect the ministry is not following the direction intended, a review is desirable. On the other hand, if the ministry seems to be progressing according to plans, the review can wait, although probably for no longer than a year. It is better to schedule a review and decide it is not needed than to overlook a review in the press of busy schedules.

The ministry review should probably include the following steps:

- Pray about the ministry and the plan. Ask God for wisdom and guidance for your work.
- Review the original vision. What was the vision for the ministry? Are you fulfilling that vision? Is the vision still the same, or has it changed since you wrote it?
- Review each objective and determine what progress, if any, has been made. Which objectives have you reached? Why? If you have not reached some objectives, what do you think has interfered with your work?
- Based on your review, do some objectives need to be revised? If so, do you need to revise only the completion date, or do you need to find a new approach?
- Keep a close eye on the system of accountability in the ministry. Do all people involved in the ministry report to someone else? On a timely basis? Are the relationships working smoothly?
- Seek new ways to improve the ministry, even if you have reached all your original objectives. You might decide now is the time to add another specific ministry to your church's prayer ministry.
- After the review, make the necessary revisions. When you do, be sure to inform all who are affected so they can make adjustments.
- Schedule the next review session.

Reviews are a time to celebrate God's grace and faithfulness and to thank God for the lives changed through the ministry. They are also a time to look honestly at the ministry and ask questions to make sure the ministry is doing what was intended. Reviews also enable us to look to the future with confidence, knowing we have asked God for guidance and are open to God's leading.

Include the following steps in your review.

Reviews are a time to celebrate.

Conclusion

God inspires in many ways.

"For surely I know the plans I have for you, says the Lord, plans for your welfare and not for harm, to give you a future with hope. Then when you call upon me and come and pray to me, I will hear you. When you search for me, you will find me; if you seek me with all your heart. I will let you find me, says the Lord, …" (Jeremiah 29:11-14).

God wants us to pray.

God inspires us to grow in our relationship with him and to minister to one another and all creation. God can inspire us in many ways. Sometimes inspiration comes in a vision, sometimes in a dream or surprising idea. God might also show someone an important, unmet need that leads to new or expanded ministries. However inspiration occurs, God calls us to action to do God's will.

Prayer is God's gift.

God has had conversations with his people from the very beginning. In Genesis, we read that God created people, blessed them, and then started to talk to them (see Genesis 1:26-28). God has wanted people to talk to him ever since, and continues to call people into fellowship with him even today. God still wants people to pray. All around the world, people are responding to God's invitation to pray. Starting a prayer ministry in your church is one response to God's call for today. "Let anyone who has an ear listen to what the Spirit is saying to the churches" (Revelation 2:7, 11, 17, 29, and 3:6, 13, and 22).

Prayer is the foundation of every Christian's relationship with God and God's gift to us. We can always turn to Jesus' invitation: "Ask, and it will be given you; search, and you will find; knock, and the door will be opened for you" (Matt. 7:7).

APPENDIX A
START-UP MINISTRIES

PRAYER FOCUS CARD

Start-Up Ministry

Synopsis

A card listing selected prayer topics is prepared and distributed—usually monthly—for interested people to use on a daily or weekly basis.

Resources Required

- Someone to select the prayer topics, type the original card, duplicate it, and distribute copies.
- Colored paper to distinguish one month's card from the next. Card stock is more resistant to wear and tear. An 8 1/2 x 11" sheet can be cut into three 3 2/3 x 8 1/2" cards, but other shapes will work.
- A paper cutter.
- Envelopes, if cards will be mailed.

Description

The prayer focus card invites individuals to join in prayer for the same concern during the same month or on the same day. Cards may be printed in or distributed with the worship bulletin or newsletter. Or they may be mailed separately to all members and friends of the church, or only to people who sign up to receive them. Recipients should be encouraged to keep the prayer focus card in a convenient place, such as on the refrigerator door, tucked into the visor in the car, on their desks, or in the Bible.

Often cards have a theme for the month, or four or five weekly themes can be used. The card may include a suggested prayer for each day of the week, to be used for four weeks. In addition, prayers for certain days may be requested. Or daily topics that fit the broader theme may be suggested.

The prayer focus card is most effective when the pastor or someone who knows the sermon topics for the month coordinates those themes with the card's prayer topics. Monthly or weekly themes might also be based on the church year and highlight Christmas, Easter, Pentecost, and less well known events such as the Week of Prayer for Christian Unity (January 18-25) or All Saints' Day (November 1).

Themes can also focus on key biblical concepts. If a biblical theme is selected, choose a verse from the Bible as the theme verse. For example, a major theme for several months could be the fruit of the Holy Spirit. Galatians 5:22-23 could be used as the theme verse, and each month could focus on one of the nine gifts: love, joy, peace, patience, kindness, generosity, faithfulness, gentleness, and self-control.

Special church and community needs can make excellent prayer themes. Cards might focus on plans to call a new pastor, an upcoming capital fund drive, the spread of the gospel at home and abroad, poverty issues, advocacy programs, general and Christian education, ecumenical endeavors, and other concerns.

You might also look for ways to connect the focus to events outside the church, for example, select "love" as the theme for February, the month of Valentine's Day. If you provide a prayer for each day of the week, on Mondays the suggested prayer could be, "Thank you, God, for your unconditional love." On Tuesdays suggest, "Lord, love someone through me today," and so on for the week.

Global hot spots and other events in the news can make good themes. Special days or public events such as Memorial Day or election day might also be noted.

You can also pray for various categories of people, such as farmers, government employees, parents, professional people, law enforcement personnel, emergency personnel, and so on.

An example of a prayer focus card is shown at right.

AUGUST PRAYER FOCUS

Theme Verse: 1 Timothy 2:1-3
"First of all, then, I urge that supplications, prayers, intercessions, and thanksgivings be made for everyone, for kings and all who are in high positions, so that we may lead a quiet and peaceable life in all godliness and dignity. This is right and is acceptable in the sight of God our Savior."

Monday
Holy Spirit, help me to find time to pray.

Tuesday
Lord, teach us to pray.

Wednesday
God of all creation, I pray for your protection for my family and all you have given me.

Thursday
Jesus, teach me to hear your voice.

Friday
Holy Spirit, show me someone I can pray for today.

Saturday
Jesus, my friend, be with me today.

Sunday
Thank you, God, for the gift of prayer. Help me to use it often.

PRAYER CALENDAR

Start-Up Ministry

Synopsis

A calendar identifying one or more prayer topics for each day of any given month or sequence of months is prepared and distributed.

Resources Required

- Someone to consult the church activity calendar and select or collect the prayer topics, type the calendar, duplicate it, and distribute copies
- Colored paper for added appeal
- Access to the church bulletin or newsletter for distribution of the prayer calendar

Description

The prayer calendar encourages recipients to make prayer a part of each day. It is also a quick and easy way to circulate many prayer concerns. Most calendars include one prayer item for each day.

Typical prayer topics include pastors and their families by name, members of church leadership groups (church council, worship committee, mission commission), individual ministries within the church, special events, special needs of the congregation, congregational goals, and so forth. Some prayer calendars also include a scripture verse for each day.

You might select a particular ministry of the church and cover all its needs on the same date each month. For example, on the tenth of each month, you could pray for the Sunday school, including the superintendent, teachers, helpers, students, the nursery, and so on. In a larger church with many different ministries and groups, you might pray for a different ministry on the tenth of each month—for the Sunday school on September 10, the stewardship committee on October 10, and so on. Or you could set up a two- or three-month rotation of prayer concerns. You might also select five to ten high-priority items to cover every month and then rotate other prayer concerns. To create more interest, rotating items can be listed on different days from month to month.

It is important to leave room for prayers about current needs. Church leaders should also have opportunities to submit prayer items for the calendar on a regular basis. High-priority needs might be listed in a special section of the calendar. See example of a prayer calendar on the next page.

Face to Face with God

JUNE PRAYER CALENDAR
Focus for Month: Peace

Special Needs

… For God's blessing on our church's ministry.

… For Sunday morning worship attendance to increase to 275.

… For our staff's physical, emotional, and spiritual well-being.

… For members to grow in their enthusiasm for our church's mission.

1 Pray for those attending the prayer ministry retreat on June 5, that they will grow in their relationship with God and their commitment to this ministry.

2 Pray for high school and college graduates as they move to their next life task.

3 Pray for protection for the high school youth group as they begin their work with Habitat for Humanity.

4 Pray that those who worship with us tomorrow will experience God's presence.

5 Pray for renewed enthusiasm for our church's greeters, ushers, and nursery attendants.

6 Pray that Christians everywhere will see how they can be faithful to God through the work they do.

7 Pray for those who struggle with addictions.

8 Pray that people will have a hunger for God's word.

9 Pray for our church office staff.

10 Pray that members of our church will be bold and invite someone to worship with them this Sunday.

11 Pray for members of our prayer ministry.

12 Pray for the Miller family as they begin a small group for teens and parents.

13 Pray for the Celebration Choir as they travel to share their gifts with churches in Illinois.

14 Pray that members of our church will find ways to share their faith through their everyday lives.

15 Pray that God's Spirit will be with our pastor as she prepares Sunday's sermon.

16 Pray that members will be eager to participate in activities at our church.

17 Pray for our preschool teachers and students and their families.

18 Pray that guests at our worship services will feel drawn into a closer relationship with God.

19 Pray for Crossover, the career transitions support group.

20 Pray for the vacation Bible school staff as they prepare for the week ahead.

21 Pray for God's love to be demonstrated through our members.

22 Pray for wisdom for members of our church council.

23 Pray that those who worship in our church will be excited to learn new things about God.

24 Pray that the Lord of the harvest will find eager workers.

25 Pray for our church's Wednesday night programs.

26 Pray that many people will be blessed by our church's community outreach.

27 Pray for our church committees and their work.

28 Pray that members and friends of our church will grow to love one another deeply.

29 Pray for those who are preparing for our church's capital fund campaign this fall.

30 Pray that members and friends of our church will grow in their relationship with God through prayer.

PRAYER LISTS *for* SPECIAL NEEDS

Start-Up Ministry

Synopsis

A collection of identified needs is prepared weekly and used by designated intercessors as a guide for prayer.

Resources Required

- Someone to collect, compile, type, and distribute the lists
- Person(s) to offer prayers for those with special needs

Description

Prayer lists are the delight of people who feel called to offer prayers of intercession. A list might be published weekly and, as appropriate, include such categories as
- those who are hospitalized
- those who are not hospitalized, but still need healing in spirit, soul, and/or body
- general, miscellaneous needs
- deaths
- births
- reports of answered prayers

Prayer lists can be very brief, usually including only a name and a short description of the need. Some people request anonymity, but usually the people requesting prayer are thankful for it and do not object to having their names used. Always be sensitive to requests for confidentiality, however. Remind those who pray that the information they receive is confidential. Consider having all participants sign a statement of confidentiality (see next page).

Prayer lists require attention to three questions.
- **What items should be placed on the list?** Generally, when someone calls the church and requests prayer, they have good reasons for doing so. Some screening might need to be done by the coordinator, but in most instances, if prayer is requested, the request should be on the list. For a mature intercessor, any prayer list is appropriate. For a newcomer, however, a lengthy list can seem overwhelming. The list should not become too long and complicated if you want broad participation in this ministry.
- **Who should receive the prayer list?** People who have been identified as intercessors are the primary recipients, but if your church has other prayer groups, group members might be asked to pray, either individually or in their groups. An often overlooked source of prayer support is homebound people. Homebound members often are eager to serve and would be more than willing to receive training to serve the church through prayer. This is an excellent way to help these members feel more a part of the church family.
- **How long should prayer items be kept on the lists?** Items should be left on the list as long as needed. Some people will call back and let you

know what has happened.
A rule of thumb, howev-
er, is to review requests
after one week and again
after thirty days. Simply
call people and ask how
things are going and if
they are still interested
in prayer support.

Face to Face with God
STATEMENT *of* CONFIDENTIALITY

Name _____

Ministry _____

Ministry Team Leader _____

As you participate in this ministry of our church, you will often hear personal information from or about people who seek our prayers. **All personal
information is confidential** and therefore may not be shared with anyone
other than the leader of your prayer ministry team or the pastor. Because we
want you to know how seriously we take this sacred trust, we ask that you
read and sign this Statement of Confidentiality.

1. I understand that all personal prayer requests received by me or others
   involved in our church's ministry of prayer are confidential.
2. I will not share with anyone, except the leader of my ministry team or
   the pastor, information I hear when receiving prayer requests as part of
   my work in this ministry.
3. I will forward all requests for prayer, other than requests for my personal
   prayers, to the leader of my ministry team or the pastor, who will decide
   how the request should be handled.
4. If I have questions about a prayer concern or an issue of confidentiality, I
   will contact the leader of my ministry team or the pastor.
5. If information that I believe is confidential is shared with me, I will
   report it immediately to the leader of my ministry team or the pastor,
   and I will keep the information confidential.

I have read and agree to abide by the provisions of this statement.

Signature _____ Date _____

Pastor or Team Leader _____ Date _____

GENERAL PRAYER CHAIN

Start-Up Ministry

Synopsis

A network of people receives prayer requests over the telephone, passes requests to others, and prays for each request.

Resources Required

- A coordinator to organize chain and recruit participants. It is wise to provide some basic training for those who are recruited.
- Someone to receive prayer requests and make the first contacts in the prayer chain on a timely basis. Both maintenance and review of the chain and requests are needed from time to time.
  Note: Depending on the size of the church, the same person might handle both tasks.

Description

A general prayer chain is a relatively simple prayer activity to organize. It is a good starting point for a prayer ministry because of its flexibility and convenience. As with many other activities, the key is finding good coordinators. A prayer chain can be established by only a few people. After a training program is developed, more members can be recruited. (Training might cover only policies and procedures of the prayer chain, or it might include a course of study on prayer with an emphasis on intercessory prayer.)

The prayer chain is activated by the coordinator, who receives the prayer request from the person who wants to be prayed for, or from the pastor, the church secretary, or another third party. Third-party requests should be screened for confidentiality before they are released. The person to be prayed for (or a contact person) should be called and asked if he or she would mind receiving prayer through the prayer chain. (Sometimes a third party will have already received permission to make a request of the prayer chain, but be cautious about accepting a third party's go-ahead. "Oh, I'm sure he wouldn't mind" is not adequate permission!)

Whether the request is direct or from a third party, the coordinator needs to find out how much information can be included in the request. Here are some basic, common sense rules.

- If practical, ask the affected person or family for permission to use the prayer chain.
- If practical, ask if the person's name may be used.
- If the person wants to maintain anonymity, you may use a made-up name, or avoid names and just describe the condition, saying something general like, "Pray for a person who entered the hospital for surgery today."

After determining in what form the request is to be presented to the chain, the coordinator passes on the request to the first available member of the prayer chain.

Every prayer chain member has a list of the other members and their telephone numbers. If the first member on the list is not available, the caller goes to the next until a person is found to receive the request. That person does three things:

- Immediately contacts the next available person on the list
- Conveys the prayer request as it was received
- Prays for the person who has requested prayer

The prayer request continues through the entire prayer chain until it comes back to the coordinator. Later the coordinator might also pass along a report about how the prayer was answered. Such reports can be a great source of encouragement to the prayer chain members.

Because confidentiality is such an important issue in prayer chains, the following measures should be taken:

- During training, stress the importance of confidentiality.
- Ask all participants to sign a simple statement of confidentiality before they enter the prayer chain (see page 49).
- Immediately after becoming aware of possible confidentiality violations, the coordinator checks to make sure he or she has all the facts and that they are clear. Then the coordinator addresses the issue with the person or persons involved. The coordinator gives a warning and makes it clear that if confidentiality is broken again, the person(s) will be asked to leave the chain.

Prayer chains can function well with as many as ten to twenty members. After that, it might be best to start a new prayer chain. It is also possible to reshape the chain into a tree. Then the coordinator might contact up to three people, each on a separate branch of the tree. These three people each pass on the request to members of their respective branches.

Larger churches might want to have separate prayer chains for mornings, afternoons, and evenings, and perhaps for every day of the week. Another idea is to develop prayer chains for individual ministries within the church. For example, you might have a prayer chain for the Sunday school, the youth ministry, the singles group, and so on.

SANCTUARY PRAYER CHAIN

Start-Up or Intermediate Ministry

Synopsis

Prayer request slips are stapled into loops and connected to form a chain, which is hung in the church sanctuary.

Resources Required

- 8 ¹/₂ x 11" colored paper, with four prayer request forms printed lengthwise on each sheet. Forms are cut apart, forming four strips.
- Someone to place the prayer request forms in the pew racks regularly.
- Someone to staple the prayer request forms together into a chain.
- A ladder or a cherry picker, so the prayer chain can be hung on hooks high enough to be out of the way of children and church activities.
- Someone to hang the chain.

Description

The sanctuary prayer chain is usually an annual event. It reminds people of the many needs we can take to God in prayer, and invites worshipers to pray for the needs of others and to encourage others to pray. Because each link is a different color, the chain also looks attractive and festive. It can easily be coordinated with another activity such as vacation church school or a month of emphasis on prayer (see page 78). The chain grows with each Sunday's new requests, which can be added before the next week's worship services.

Start-Up Ministry

During the announcements, the pastor encourages worshipers to fill out a prayer request form and place it in the offering plate, or leave it in the pew to be collected by volunteers or ushers. At the same time, the pastor can briefly explain that the prayer chain is a special reminder to pray and to encourage others to pray (in keeping with the emphasis on prayer that month, if that is the case).

Intermediate Ministry

If your church is ready for an intermediate ministry, it would certainly be appropriate to recruit intercessors to pray every day during the emphasis for the prayer chain requests. One intercessor might pray for the requests each day. Some might pray in the sanctuary, others at home.

The prayer chain ministry can be expanded. For example, keeping in mind that prayer request forms represent many of the felt needs of the congregation, you might separate the forms into "need groups." The identified needs can then be addressed in sermons, Bible studies, and special small groups. Continued follow-up prayer may be offered for these needs. Reviewing the prayer request forms can sensitize pastors, leaders, and others to the congregation's needs.

Another possibility is to invite all the intercessors to a prayer gathering at the end of the prayer emphasis. The prayer chain can be taken apart and several forms given to each intercessor. Especially challenging prayer concerns might be set aside and prayed for by all the intercessors at the end of the prayer time. After the prayers have been offered, pray-ers might enjoy food and fellowship, too.

It is, of course, very important to maintain confidentiality at all times regarding the content of the prayer request forms.

PRAYER REQUEST

Your name

If you want the pastor or a prayer team member to send a letter to the person for whom we are praying, write on the reverse side of this slip the name and address of the person who should receive the letter.

☐ your request **may** be read to the congregation
☐ your request **will not** be read to the congregation

NATIONAL DAY *of* PRAYER

Start-Up or Intermediate Ministry

Synopsis

Abraham Lincoln was the first president to designate the first Thursday in May as a day to pray for the United States of America.

Resources Required

The National Day of Prayer may be observed in different ways. Depending on the level of involvement you select, resources required will vary considerably. The National Day of Prayer Task Force has literature with many helpful suggestions. You can write to the task force at P.O. Box 15616, Colorado Springs, CO 80935-5616.

Description

Your church's observance of the National Day of Prayer may be as simple or complex as you choose. You might simply include a notice in the church bulletin announcing the day and encouraging members and guests to pray for the country and its leaders that day. You might organize an ecumenical prayer breakfast for churches in your neighborhood. (See page 76 for suggestions.) If your church is ready for an advanced prayer ministry, you can organize a community-wide gathering at the state capitol or city hall.

Start-Up Ministry

A simple way to observe the National Day of Prayer is to invite people to take a break at noon and pray. Put together a prayer list that people can pick up in church the preceding Sunday, or distribute the list with the bulletin. The list could include specific requests for national, state, and local government officials, schools, and churches, as well as general requests for teachers, students, families, and others. Encourage participants to take time during their lunch breaks to pray about the items on the list.

Intermediate Ministry

A somewhat more involved observance might be built around a Prayer for the Nation meeting at noon on the National Day of Prayer. Announce the observance on the two preceding Sundays. Also include an invitation in the bulletin and/or church newsletter.

Prepare a list of items to be covered during the prayer time. This list can include general prayers for protection, direction, and blessing for the country; the president and his family, advisors, and staff; the Congress; the Supreme Court; the governor and his or her advisors; the state legislature; the state supreme court; the judicial system; law enforcement agencies; the mayor and city council; schools and those involved in education; business and commerce communities; the medical community; cultural organizations; poor, homeless, and oppressed people; and other individuals, groups, organizations, and institutions. Here is a simple agenda.

- Welcome and greetings
- A brief explanation of the purpose of the meeting

- Instructions to the participants:
  - If more than five to eight people are participating, ask them to form pairs or groups of three or four.
  - Give each participant the prepared prayer list.
  - Each group or individual can choose to pray either aloud or silently. If anyone selects silent prayer, make sure to allow adequate time for them to pray.
  - Indicate how many items you want each person to cover in prayer. For example, if there are twenty items on the list and each group has four members, each participant would take five items. Group members might pray consecutively, each person taking one item and then moving to the next person.
- A hymn or song
- The Lord's Prayer
- A blessing

STAFF PRAYER

Start-Up Ministry

Synopsis   A scheduled time, usually daily or weekly, is set aside by the church staff for praying together.

Resources Required   Someone to coordinate schedules, times, and places to meet.

Description   The pastor usually makes the decision to start a prayer meeting for the staff. Some church staffs have daily devotions or prayer time. Others meet on a weekly basis.

Keep prayer meetings brief. Fifteen minutes is adequate for daily meetings, although they can be a little longer if the staff meets less frequently. Invite each staff member in turn to lead a meeting, so the task does not become overwhelming for one person, and everyone has a chance to pray over a period of days or weeks.

A short but relevant reading can be a great lead-in to the prayer time. Perhaps an appropriate hymn or song can be sung. Focus on staff and congregational needs, but incorporate other prayer requests and reports about answers to prayer. The meeting might conclude with the Lord's Prayer, a hymn or song, or a special blessing for each person, such as: "May God bless you today with *(peace, joy, courage, friendly interactions, and so on).*"

PRAYER OUTREACH

Start-Up Ministry

This enjoyable activity is designed to bring new people into prayer by combining prayer with social or athletic activities.

Synopsis

• Someone who can talk about prayer in a nonthreatening way
• Someone who likes to organize and promote fun activities
• Someone to organize car pools or rent buses, as needed
• Someone to lead short day or evening outings
Note: These tasks might be done by one person or shared by two or more people.

Resources Required

Prayer outreaches introduce people to prayer in a nonthreatening, low-key way. Some people think prayer is boring, an activity for those with nothing else to do. One way the church can combat such attitudes is to provide opportunities for novices and others to pray and have fun during a single event.

Description

Our church hosts "Prayer from the Mountain." The prayer ministry arranges a trip to Mt. Aggassiz near Flagstaff, Arizona. The trip includes a spectacular chair lift ride to to a spot overlooking the areas to the west of Flagstaff and north toward the Grand Canyon. Participants climb the last stretch, to an altitude of nearly 12,000 feet, where they enjoy the scenery, share thoughts about prayer, and pray briefly together. The trip concludes with a picnic.

Another popular activity is a pool volleyball prayer party. Sometime during the middle of the match, the group takes a break for prayer and discussion. Participants have a good time and also learn something about prayer.

If many of the participants are new to prayer, you might want to spend most of the prayer time in discussion. Stimulating questions to talk about might include
  • How do you feel about prayer?
  • What does prayer mean to you?
  • Does God answer prayers? How?

Prayer outreach activities can be a good way to bring new people into the prayer ministry. Such activities might even give a boost to current participants who feel weary after years of work with the ministry.

APPENDIX B
INTERMEDIATE MINISTRIES

PRAYER COORDINATOR

Intermediate Ministry

Synopsis

A member of the church organizes, schedules, and provides general leadership for the church's prayer activities.

Resources Required

A mature Christian who is experienced in prayer and willing to lead.

Description

Appointing and publicly recognizing a prayer coordinator is vital for any church that wants to establish a separate prayer ministry. Appointing a coordinator

- signals to the church that prayer is important
- brings attention to the ministry
- ensures that prayer has an intentional place in the church
- ensures that the ministry will not fade or be forgotten
- provides a way to recruit ministry participants and to encourage greater participation in prayer

A prayer coordinator does not need to be an expert on prayer ministry. Rather than looking for an expert, look for these qualities in the prayer coordinator:

- Christian maturity and a good reputation
- A strong prayer and devotional life
- A love for people and the ability to get along well with others
- A servant's heart
- Gifts of encouragement, organization, leadership
- Time to devote to developing, implementing, and maintaining the prayer ministry
- Understanding and acceptance of the vision and goals of the church
- Support for and from the church's leaders

If needed, one of the first tasks of the prayer coordinator should be to establish a resource library on prayer. The coordinator might begin by conducting an inventory of resources available in the church, among the members, and in the marketplace (books, videos, audiocassettes, flyers, brochures, pamphlets).

Over time, the prayer coordinator needs to develop a prayer strategy for the church, encouraging and training people in the following areas:

- Personal growth in prayer
- Small-group prayer ministries
- Corporate or open prayer ministries
- Churchwide prayer ministries
- Community prayer participation

Together with the pastor, the prayer coordinator gives energy and direction to the church's prayer organization.

Appendix B

PRAYER TAPE MINISTRY

Intermediate Ministry

Cassette tapes with a message about prayer are prepared to provide inspiration and encouragement to pray.

Synopsis

Resources Required

- The pastor, or someone the pastor designates, to select topics or themes, write scripts, and record the messages
- Someone to oversee the distribution system
- Someone with knowledge of recording equipment to organize and direct the technical portion of the ministry
- Materials and equipment
  - a quality tape recorder
  - a good microphone for sound reproduction
  - master cassette tapes of good quality for tape reproduction
  - access to a duplicating machine
  - cassette tapes for reproducing recordings

Note: If the church currently has a tape ministry, most of the technical requirements are probably already in place and can be used by the prayer tape ministry.

Description

This prayer opportunity requires more technical resources than some others, but for those with the appropriate gifts, it can be a great way to get people involved in prayer. Each tape might include the following elements:
- A brief greeting.
- A biblical text focused on the selected theme.
- A short devotion based on the theme and text.
- A prayer based on the devotion.
- Encouragement for listeners to pray about the theme or text discussed. You could lead them in a prayer they would repeat after you. Such a prayer can help people feel more comfortable praying.

The prayer tape ministry can be an important way to reach out to homebound members and friends of the church. It can also help busy people find time to listen to an inspirational message and to pray, whether daily, weekly, or occasionally. Many people will probably choose to listen to these tapes while driving to and from work.

To start out, prepare tapes monthly. The number of messages will depend on length of message, time available for production, resources, and so on. Tapes for homebound recipients are mailed, of course, but tapes can also be distributed on Sunday morning. A box with new tapes can be placed in or near the sanctuary or main traffic corridors. Next to it, place another box for returned tapes. Recycling tapes will keep expenses down. You might also add a box for contributions to defray the cost of production.

PRAYER VIGIL

Intermediate Ministry

Synopsis

A vigil provides a significant period of focused time for continuous prayer, usually on one specific topic.

Resources Required

- Someone to organize, promote, and recruit participants for the event
- A guide for participants with general information and instructions, timetables, selected scripture verses, and prayer topics
- A convenient place to pray if the vigil is conducted in the church and not in homes

Description

A prayer vigil is a time set aside for prayer and meditation, usually focused on one or several specific topics. It can be a concentrated time of prayer about an upcoming church project, such as the stewardship drive, Christmas or Holy Week preparation, a special workshop or conference, or other events. Or a vigil can be broader in scope, addressing even national or international conflicts or needs. Your church might hold a vigil once a year or as often as every two or three months.

The prayer vigil guide (possibly as short as one page) includes general information about what a prayer vigil is, how it works, and what is expected of each participant. It is good to include some verses from the Bible about being vigilant and God's faithfulness and attentiveness to us. Instructions about time and place are also important if the guide will be sent out to participants ahead of time. Some guides for prayer vigils also include a suggested procedure for the time of prayer, including ideas about how to prepare body and mind for prayer; readings or hymns of praise to God; lists of things a person might pray about; litanies or other possible formats for offering petitions; and closing hymns, readings, prayers, or blessings. (See pages 64 and 65 for sample.)

The heart of the guide, however, is the section with suggested prayer topics. Generally, include enough items to guide participants for at least the period of time they have volunteered for, usually an hour or half hour. If you are starting out, you might consider half-hour intervals, which will be less intimidating.

Time intervals are also somewhat determined by the length of the prayer vigil and the number of people you want to involve. For example, if your vigil is six hours, it might be better to use half-hour or even quarter-hour segments to increase participation. Another way to involve more people during a six-hour vigil would be to organize group prayer times or to ask participants to pray in their homes. (Some churches offer a choice between praying at church or at home, especially if the vigil goes through the night.)

An interesting possibility that allows you to have a longer vigil even though you might not have many participants from your own church is to find prayer partners in other locations who might want to join you. You could even connect with prayer partners in other parts of the world, especially during the night when it is hard to find participants.

It is important to make reminder calls to participants on the day before the vigil. Sometimes during vigils, individual participants call the next member of the vigil before stopping their own prayer time. This is an excellent way to ensure continuity of prayer.

PRAYER REQUESTS
Prayer Vigil for World Peace

Those who keep the prayer vigil will offer prayers on behalf of the whole community. You may request prayers

    … *of thankfulness*
    … *for help and guidance*
    … *for God's presence and blessing*
    … *for strength and support*
    … *for health and wholeness*
    … *for a friend or loved one who is struggling*
    … *of concern regarding your life, our community, or the world situation*

Please write your requests below and place this sheet in the offering plate, or hand it to an usher or to our pastor. You may make as many requests as you like.

PRAYER VIGIL *for* WORLD PEACE

Enter the church, even though the previous person may still be praying.
Use any of this material as you wish. It is offered only as a suggestion.

As you enter the church, pray that God will be with you during this vigil.
    Ever-present God, I am in your house. Help me to keep my thoughts on you, that I may hear you speaking in my heart and know your peace. Amen.

Be seated in one of the pews and pray:
    Faithful God, you are near to those who call upon you. You have promised that whatever we ask in faith we shall receive. Make me bold to ask and eager to praise and serve you, in the name of Jesus Christ. Amen.

In silence, let your eyes explore the sanctuary. Pray:
    O how blessed is this place, filled with solace, light, and grace.

Offer a prayer of confession:
    Gracious God, I have prayed so often for peace. But I forget that as one of your children, I am called to be a peacemaker. I think most often about my desire that others be peaceful toward me, and I have nurtured prejudice, anger, resentment, and even hatred against others. Forgive me for my contribution toward violence in the world. Let me become a healer of those who are the victims of hatred. In Christ's name, Amen.

Take a Bible into your hands. Let your eyes rest upon it and pray:
    God-with-us, as I prepare to read your word, give me a heart made ready by your Spirit. By your grace, let me receive and understand your truth, and lead me to serve you with all my heart and soul, strength and mind. Shine on me, true Light of all. Amen.

Read several Bible passages or hymn texts.
    Suggested Bible readings: Psalm 147, Ecclesiastes 3:1-8, John 4:27, Philippians 4:6, 7
    Suggested hymns: "O God of Love, O King of Peace" (414); "O God of Every Nation" (416)

Pray for the church. Here are several suggestions.
- Use your own words.
- Use the Prayers for Peace on page 42 of *Lutheran Book of Worship*, or use any of the prayers on pages 42-51.
- Pray for the whole church of Christ.
- Pray for our congregation, asking God to give each of our members a spirit of servanthood.
- Pray that all members will be faithful in worship and prayer.
- Pray for those who do not know Christ, using your own words or the words of hymn 388, "O Spirit of the Living God."
- Pray for our pastor, using the words of hymn 286, "Bow Down Your Ear, Almighty God."

Pray for all people according to their needs. Again, here are several suggestions.
- Pray for unity in Christ and for the peace of the whole world.
- Pray for specific situations in the world where there is no peace.
- Pray for the sick and homebound.
- Pray for those who grieve.
- Pray for those who are in danger or trouble.
- Pray, as you are led, for your family and loved ones, for personal problems, for health.
- Pray for those who have no one to pray for them.

Now for several minutes, simply be still in God's presence. Begin by praying:

God of silence, in my daily life I have contributed much to the world's noise and confusion. Help me now to be still and to know your peace, that you are God, and that in quietness I will find your strength. *(silence)*

End the silence by praying:

Amen. Lord, you have commanded us to pray, and you have promised to hear us for Jesus' sake. Amen.

Offer a prayer of personal commitment.
First, leave your pew and stand before the baptismal font, and pray:

Loving God, I stand here to honor the greatest event in my life. It was through baptism that I became your child and an heir to everlasting life. Be with me and all the baptized, that we may rise each day to new life in you. Amen.

Then move to the pulpit and pray:

God of all creation, you came to us in the Word made flesh, your son Jesus Christ, and you come to us again and again in the words of Scripture and the preaching of the gospel. I have not always been attentive to your word, and I do not always live according to your commands. By your Spirit, make me eager to hear and obey your word. Amen.

Finally, kneel before the altar and pray:

Glory to you, Holy God. I have come before your altar many times to receive your body and blood, your forgiveness. Even though I often do things that break my relationship with you, you love me and keep calling me. I come before you now to commit myself to your will, so that I may be a witness to your eternal peace. Fill my heart and mind with a desire to be wholly dedicated to your service. In Jesus' name, Amen.

In silence, recall God's many blessings to you and give thanks.

Return to a pew and pray:

Prince of Peace, help all your people to discover what it means to follow you. Help us to settle the conflicts in our hearts, so that peace may be personal, as well as international. Give us cause for joyous living. For the sake of the one who is the source of all peace, Jesus Christ, Amen.

Pray the Lord's Prayer.

PRAYER RETREAT *or* SEMINAR

Intermediate Ministry

Synopsis   These gatherings focus on general prayer or a particular aspect of prayer.

Resources Required
- Someone, probably a committee, to organize the retreat or seminar for the church.
- Someone to lead the event.
- Money for an honorarium for the speaker, brochures, promotion, and rental of a meeting facility, as required. (Ideally, these expenses are covered by a fee charged to participants. Usually, however, some seed money is needed to get the project off the ground.)

Description   Prayer retreats and seminars take significant amounts of energy, but they can get your prayer ministry off to an excellent start. Such events create momentum and enthusiasm for prayer.

Planning is critical to a successful event. Make sure the event is put on the church calendar early (six to twelve months in advance), to avoid conflicts with other church activities and to give people the opportunity to make plans to attend. If you have never planned a retreat or seminar, try to find someone with experience to advise you.

If your church has a prayer coordinator, that person, together with the pastor and other appropriate church leaders, can start by
- appointing an organizing committee
- selecting a date for the event
- deciding on a workable budget
- convening the organizing committee and deciding who should lead the first meeting

For our purposes in this handbook, the difference between a retreat and a seminar has to do with duration and location. A retreat usually takes place away from the church, perhaps at a retreat center or someplace where participants can get away for a while. Retreats tend to be more involved, longer, and more relaxing. Seminars are usually shorter but more intense, and more often are held in a local church. If you have not organized such an event before, it might be wise to start with a Saturday seminar from 9:00 A.M. to 2:00 P.M. in your own building. Short, local events are less expensive and more convenient.

As you organize your retreat or seminar, keep the following areas of responsibility in mind:
- **Purpose.** Define the purpose of the retreat or seminar.
- **Prayer.** Ask someone to organize prayer support for the planning and implementation of the event.
- **Volunteers.** Decide how many you will need to recruit and train.
- **Program.** Organize the details of the program, including arranging for a speaker. You might include sessions on topics such as how to develop a

personal prayer life, prayer and evangelism, intercession, healing prayer, meditation, and spiritual growth.

- **Promotion.** You need to get the word out.
- **Registration.** Someone needs to help with preregistration, fee collection, registration during the event, and so on.
- **Lodging and meal arrangements, if needed.** Consider church camps, motels, bed-and-breakfasts, private homes, and so on. Keep in mind the size of your group, the type and number of spaces needed for the entire group and for small discussion groups to meet, space for worship, meals, sleeping, quiet time, and play time. If you are holding a seminar in your own church, participants might bring lunches, or another group in the church might be willing to prepare lunch.
- **Transportation, if needed.** Buses or car pools might be needed for events away from the church.

After your event, review and record your experiences. Good records can be a real boost for next year's organizing committee.

Open Prayer Meeting

Intermediate Ministry

Synopsis

Open prayer meetings are open to the public. People gather mainly to pray and to enjoy fellowship.

Resources Required

- Someone, perhaps the prayer coordinator, to organize and promote the meeting and to recruit participants.
- Someone with a creative flair to design invitations.
- People to make personal invitations, by word of mouth and in writing.
- Ideally, a meeting place in which interruptions are kept to a minimum. If no private rooms are available, the church sanctuary can be used; prayer can be offered around the altar. However, a private room is usually more comfortable, convenient, and conducive to fellowship.

Description

Open, or corporate, prayer meetings are usually conducted in the church. The program format varies depending on size, purpose, intended participants, and other factors. Following is a possible program, designed to keep focus and direction clear.

- **Welcome.** State the reason for coming together.
- **Icebreaker.** Provide a way for participants to get better acquainted.
- **Worship.** At a minimum, include one or more hymns or songs and a brief prayer.
- **Scripture reading.** Begin to focus on the meeting's purpose.
- **Silent reflection or listening prayer.** Each participant records whatever comes to mind.
- **Prayer time.** Based on the announced purpose of the meeting, items recorded during listening prayer, presented needs, and other requests are offered. Participants may pray individually or in small groups, silently or aloud, as they are inclined, but groups that choose to pray out loud should try not to disturb others.
- **Closing.** Perhaps a hymn or song is sung, or the Lord's Prayer is prayed together. Also thank people for coming and invite them back.
- **Fellowship time.** Extend an invitation for those who want to stay.

Make sure that open prayer meetings are inviting to newcomers, so people will return and bring others. Ask yourself, Who am I trying to reach? The answer might be, everyone in the church, or all Christians in our neighborhood. However, larger churches might take advantage of the fact that people enjoy coming together with others like them: young people with other young people, parents with other parents. A larger church could offer a group primarily for retired people or for young parents (offering the parents nursery care during the meeting).

Also ask, What is my purpose for having an open prayer meeting? You might offer meetings to pray for a variety of concerns. For example, on Wednesdays at noon, the open prayer meeting could focus on praying for the world. Certain countries could be adopted for prayer. Bring in maps and lay hands on the selected countries. Invite guests who can talk about the country, its gifts, and its needs. Such a meeting is particularly attractive to people with interest in missions.

On Thursdays, the focus could be healing prayer. People who have special health needs could come to receive individual prayers for healing of spirit, soul, and body. When people are hurting, they are often more open to prayer support. And many come back to pray for others who are struggling, after they themselves have been restored to health and peace.

On Sunday mornings before the services start, a meeting might be held for the church's members, worship services, classes, and programs. Participants will include those who find it convenient to come to church a little earlier, and who like the opportunity to pray specifically for the church.

Opportunities are plentiful. Be creative. Ask God to show you people's needs. Then design a way, through open prayer meetings, to meet those needs.

PRAYER SMALL GROUP

Intermediate Ministry

Synopsis

A small group of members and friends meeting in a home to learn about prayer and to pray.

Resources Required

- Someone to lead the first small group. It's helpful to provide some training in small group dynamics.
- People to promote this opportunity to the church. Recruiting group members is best accomplished through personal invitations, but any means will be helpful.
- Money, if, for example, you want to purchase a study on prayer for the group members, or if you want to buy hymnals or song books.

Description

The prayer small group is different from any other small group only in its focus on prayer. The focus depends on the group and the vision God has given the ministry's leaders. Group members need to have input on the final decision. A group might focus on any of the following:
- A Bible study on prayer
- A discussion group based on one or more prayer topics
- Instruction for new pray-ers on how to pray
- Prayer for the members of the group and their families
- Prayer for the church, leadership, members, and so forth
- Prayer for specific needs
- A combination of two or more of the above

Small groups are great places for developing leaders. When each group is organized, give responsibilities to as many people as possible. For example:
- Leader (selected before the group is started)
- Assistant leader (leads when the leader is absent and hones developing skills)
- Host (provides a home for the meetings)
- Hospitality and refreshments leader
- Worship leader (brings the hymnals or song books, leads the singing)
- Teacher (if someone other than the leader)
- Arrangements person (calls members about upcoming meetings, and so forth)

If your church already has a small group ministry, consider participating in the general training. Then add specialized training for your prayer ministry. If you are starting a prayer small group with people new to church, the following progression might be useful for each meeting:
- Discussion about personal experiences with and questions about prayer
- Study of prayer
- Prayer

This development is gradual and nonthreatening, its pace determined by the group members' growth and readiness. Be especially sensitive to members who are reluctant to pray out loud. Keep in mind, however, that the purpose of the group is to pray.

Bookstores and some organizations offer excellent resources, including seminars, on small group organization, development, and motivation. Take advantage of training opportunities when available.

See other materials in this *Face to Face with God* series.

Baranowski, Arthur B. *Creating Small Faith Communities: A Plan for Restructuring the Parish and Renewing Catholic Life.* Cincinnati: St. Anthony Messenger Press, 1988.

Foster, Richard J. and James Bryan Smith, eds. *Devotional Classics: Selected Readings for Individuals and Groups.* San Francisco: Harper San Francisco, 1992.

Foster, Richard J. *Freedom from Simplicity* and *Freedom from Simplicity: Leader's Guide.* San Francisco: Harper San Francisco, 1989.

Foster, Richard J. *Prayer: Finding the Heart's True Home.* San Francisco: Harper San Francisco, 1992.

Galloway, Dale E. *20/20 Vision.* Portland, OR: Scott Publishing Company, 1990.

Gorman, Julie A. *Community That Is Christian: A Handbook on Small Groups.* Wheaton, IL: Victor Books, 1993.

Icenogle, Gareth Weldon. *Biblical Foundations for Small Group Ministry: An Intergenerational Approach.* Downers Grove, IL: InterVarsity Press, 1994.

Klug, Lyn. *Praying: Meeting God in Daily Life.* Minneapolis: Augsburg Fortress, 1995.

Lavin, Ronald J. *You Can Grow in a Small Group.* Lima, Ohio: C.S.S. Publishing Company, Inc., 1976.

Morgan, Henry, ed. *Approaches to Prayer: A Resource Book for Groups and Individuals.* Ridgefield, CT: 1993.

Price, Richard, Pat Springle, and Joe Kloba. *Rapha's Handbook for Group Leaders.* Houston: Rapha Publishing, 1991.

Smith, James Bryan. *A Spiritual Formation Workbook: Small Group Resources for Nurturing Christian Growth.* San Francisco: Harper San Francisco, 1993.

Starting Small Groups—and Keeping Them Going. Minneapolis: Augsburg Fortress, 1995.

Vest, Norvene. *Bible Reading for Spiritual Growth.* San Francisco: Harper San Francisco, 1993.

Webb, Lance. *The Art of Personal Prayer.* Nashville: Abingdon, 1992.

Resources for Prayer Small Groups

MEMBERSHIP INTERCESSION MINISTRY

Intermediate or Advanced Ministry

Synopsis   A ministry to pray for and, sometimes, to contact every member of the church.

Resources Required
- Someone to coordinate the ministry and, if desired, to recruit others to pray regularly for the members
- A copy of or access to the current church membership list

Description   The main purpose of this ministry is to provide prayer support for all church members. It can be expanded to include regular contact with members.

Intermediate Ministry   To begin, an intercessor prays regularly for the church members, perhaps for one or two hours each week. The intercessor might work with an alphabetic membership list, keeping a check-in and check-out log to record progress. Prayers might be offered for protection, direction, blessings from God, good health, more frequent attendance at church, deeper commitment to Christ, and a desire to pray.

The ministry can be expanded by sending a letter to every person or family prayed for, informing them that they were prayed for that day. The letter could include a little note of appreciation for being part of the church family. People are usually pleased to receive a letter from the church that doesn't request money or ask them to usher on Sunday morning. Such letters sometimes bring inactive members back to church and encourage greater involvement from others.

Advanced Ministry   The letter could include a tear-off section at the bottom that the recipient could use for written prayer requests. This option requires some extra work: preparing letters, keeping track of the returned prayer request forms, making sure that someone prays for what is requested. It is well worth the extra effort. You might consider taking the membership intercession ministry yet another step by using the letter to do some research about how people feel about your church. Along with the prayer request form, add one or two short, leading questions such as, "What do you like best about our church?" or "How can our church serve you better?" Periodically pass on responses to church staff and leaders for review and follow-up. A copy of a letter with a prayer request form is shown on the next page.

The membership intercession ministry becomes an advanced ministry when it includes a personal telephone contact program. Either instead of, or in addition to, sending a letter, someone calls and talks with the members who have recently been prayed for. Obviously more people are needed to handle this task.

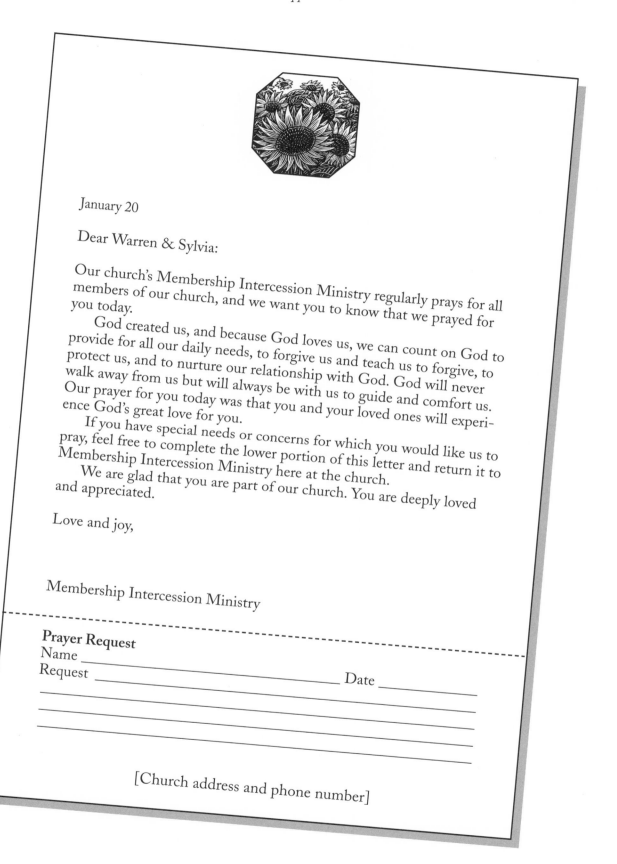

January 20

Dear Warren & Sylvia:

Our church's Membership Intercession Ministry regularly prays for all members of our church, and we want you to know that we prayed for you today.

God created us, and because God loves us, we can count on God to provide for all our daily needs, to forgive us and teach us to forgive, to protect us, and to nurture our relationship with God. God will never walk away from us but will always be with us to guide and comfort us. Our prayer for you today was that you and your loved ones will experience God's great love for you.

If you have special needs or concerns for which you would like us to pray, feel free to complete the lower portion of this letter and return it to Membership Intercession Ministry here at the church.

We are glad that you are part of our church. You are deeply loved and appreciated.

Love and joy,

Membership Intercession Ministry

- -

Prayer Request

Name _____

Request _____ Date _____
_____
_____
_____

[Church address and phone number]

PRAYERWALKING

Intermediate Ministry

Synopsis

Prayerwalkers do just that—walk around neighborhoods and pray for the area and residents.

Resources Required

- Someone to plan and implement the prayerwalk.
- Someone to recruit participants.
- A guide explaining what a prayerwalk is, how it works, and what is expected of each participant. An excellent reference is *Prayerwalking: Praying On Site with Insight* by Steve Hawthorne and Graham Kendrick (Altamonte Springs, FL: Creation House, 1993).
- Someone to arrange transportation to and from the selected neighborhoods.

Description

Prayerwalking is a ministry of intercession for neighborhoods. Today it is done all over the world, but it has its roots in Acts, which describes Christians preparing for public ministry as they walk and pray. In Norway, centuries later, reformer Hans Nielsen Hauge frequently walked while he prayed in preparation for upcoming evangelistic meetings.

Prayerwalking can range from one person praying while exercising in the morning to a group walking through a selected neighborhood. Preparations vary accordingly. Typically, prayerwalkers go in pairs or small groups. They may walk a few minutes or several hours.

Anyone able to walk or use a wheelchair can participate. Prayerwalking, popular with families, can be
- a prayer project
- an exercise opportunity
- a family outing
- a social trip with a purpose
- a time to "smell the roses" and be outside
- a chance to get together with other church members while achieving various objectives

Here are the steps you will probably need to take.
- **Determine the purpose of the prayerwalk.** It might be to pray for salvation, repentance, reconciliation, an end to violence, strengthening families, protection, blessing for people, schools, businesses, neighborhoods, and so forth.
- **Select a format for the prayerwalk.** Participants might walk alone, in pairs, as families, in small groups, in large groups.
- **Decide on the place or places for the walk.** Walks can be held in local neighborhoods, workplaces, schools, churches, overlooks, sites of troubling, evil, or tragic events.

- **Decide how to prepare the prayerwalkers.** Once the walkers have assembled, you might follow this plan.
  - Pray together.
  - Divide walkers into teams.
  - Give each person a statement of the prayerwalk's purpose or a list of prayer topics.
  - Give each team a map, if necessary.
  - Give final instructions before departure.
- Take the teams to your drop-off and pick-up points, specifying a time when the teams are to meet again.
- Do the prayerwalking.
- Return to the church or other starting point. Wrap up the event with these steps:
  - Record on a map all the places walkers covered.
  - Discuss experiences and observations.
  - Conclude with a prayer.

PRAYER BREAKFAST

Intermediate or Advanced Ministry

Synopsis

This prayer meeting conducted at breakfast time may be a regular annual, monthly, or weekly event.

Resources Required

If the breakfast is a weekly or monthly event:
- A coordinator or small group to arrange a meeting place (such as a local restaurant), contact the members and remind them of the next meeting time, extend invitations to potential new members, and either lead the meeting or secure a speaker.

If the breakfast is an annual event:
- One person, such as the prayer coordinator, or (preferably) a committee to plan and carry out the event.
- Seed money. Tickets will need to be sold unless the church or an outside sponsor is willing to finance the event. For some free publicity, a sponsor might be willing to do so.

Description

Whether they are held weekly or annually, prayer breakfasts are especially suitable for working people, assuming they end early enough for participants to get to work on time. Regularly scheduled breakfasts can be held once a month, at least in the beginning. Some groups find after getting together for a while that they are eager to meet more often.

Intermediate Ministry

For regular weekly or monthly prayer breakfasts, the key is to put together an event people enjoy attending. Fellowship and prayer are the basic elements. The prayer can be simple—people might offer only one sentence, if that is what they are comfortable with.

Depending on your resources, regular prayer breakfast meetings can also be expanded to include special music, guest speakers, individual stories about experiences with prayer, and other features. Some prayer breakfasts are built around a Bible study on prayer, followed by a time of prayer. You might want to invite a speaker who incorporates a time for discussion, which tends to get people more involved.

Advanced Ministry

For a major annual event, the committee can organize around four key activities.
- Promoting the event
- Decorating the event facility (if appropriate)
- Making food arrangements (hiring a caterer or forming a team to do the cooking)
- Devising the program (speaker, special music, and so forth)

Each task can easily by done by one person, unless your event is to be citywide.

If you decide to arrange a community prayer breakfast, generate greater participation by inviting a speaker well known in your community. Prayer breakfasts are also good opportunities to cooperate with other churches. Take the initiative and contact one or more churches to participate. Then, for example, three churches can together sponsor a prayer breakfast on the National Day of Prayer, and one church can assume responsibility for the food, another for the decorations, the third for the program. Such functions can be inspirational and sources of unity and harmony within the local body of believers. They also provide a great focus for prayer and a reminder of its importance.

Following is a format for a more involved prayer breakfast.

- Welcome and introduction of head table (if there is one)
- Table prayer
- Breakfast, during which music can be played or performed
- Special music with prayer as the theme
- A poem or story about prayer
- A message on prayer from the speaker
- A general prayer on a predetermined theme or on topics of national or community interest, such as the president, Congress, Supreme Court, governor, state legislature, state supreme court, schools, law enforcement agencies, and so on
- The Lord's Prayer

The focus of an annual prayer breakfast can be on the event speaker's message, prayer for a particular issue, or a special feature such as a personal story about faith and prayer. If the purpose of the meeting is prayer, the highlight should either bring attention to prayer or actually involve participants in prayer. If you want participants to pray, you might ask them to form small groups for prayer. Be sure you have a good sense about what style of prayer the group members are comfortable with. A time of guided silent prayer might be a better way to proceed if you are uncertain about this or know that many in the group are not accustomed to praying spontaneously with other people.

If your church would like to sponsor a larger or communitywide prayer breakfast, it might be a good idea to try a smaller event for a year or two to gain some valuable experience. However, if the church has much experience in arranging large banquets, and the necessary resources, you can move forward, asking first for God's guidance.

Appendix B

PRAYER EMPHASIS WEEK *or* MONTH

Intermediate or Advanced Ministry

Synopsis

A period of time is set aside by the church to reflect on the importance of prayer, to provide opportunities for prayer, and to invite God's spirit to make prayer more intentional for the entire church.

Resources Required

- An organizing committee, which probably includes the pastor, a representative from the prayer ministry (perhaps the prayer coordinator), and two or three others. The committee needs to select activities, schedule speakers, locate materials, and publicize the opportunity.
- Money, ideally provided through the normal budget process.

Description

A church's prayer emphasis can be a sermon on prayer or a month-long celebration. Integrating the prayer activities into the normal life of the church ensures greater participation. The committee will want to begin by seeking God's guidance about direction, timing, and so forth.

Next, the committee needs to determine the project's scope and duration. It is important to begin planning the prayer emphasis well in advance, although, of course, the less complicated the emphasis, the less planning time is needed. When determining the shape of the emphasis, the planning committee will want to take into account God's guidance and direction in prayer, resources available for the project, and the size of the current prayer ministry in the church (a clue about how many people can be expected to participate and in what manner).

Intermediate Ministry

If your church has never had a prayer emphasis before, it might be wise to choose two or three well-planned activities during a week. For example, a beginning program for a prayer emphasis week could consist of

- a Sunday morning sermon on prayer
- a Bible study on prayer, including time for prayer, over two Sundays
- developing and distributing a prayer focus card that people can use at home during the week

This kind of program is relatively easy to organize and implement. If the planners feel somewhat more ambitious and think the church is ready for more prayer-focused activity, they could add a Wednesday evening gathering, maybe a time of corporate prayer.

Advanced Ministry

A prayer emphasis ministry can vary greatly in scope. Each church needs to determine what fits its needs the best. Some churches choose a week of evening events emphasizing prayer and spiritual growth. The church's own pastor might lead these, or an outside speaker familiar with prayer (and possibly prayer ministry) might be invited to lead a series of lectures, workshops, or other activities on prayer or a particular area of prayer (intercession, healing prayer, and so forth).

Other elements churches might add to this basic emphasis include a Saturday seminar on prayer, or a Sunday night prayer meeting asking God to inspire members and friends to seek a deeper relationship with God through prayer and the ministry of the church.

If the church selects a prayer emphasis month, consider opening the month with a prayer vigil. A series of four sermons on prayer can be offered, and worshipers can request prayer using the sanctuary prayer chain format (see page 52). The Bible study can be four sessions instead of two. Open prayer meetings can be added. It might be a good idea to add one or two prayer outreach events to the schedule as well.

PRAYER CARE MINISTRY

Intermediate Ministry

Synopsis

This ministry focuses on people who are homebound or hospitalized, providing fellowship and prayer, and perhaps serving Holy Communion.

Resources Required

- A leader who can recruit and train lay people to become care ministers
- A training program for participants
- Money to purchase one or more portable Communion sets (including a sturdy card with a brief order for Holy Communion printed on it) and miscellaneous supplies

Description

A prayer care ministry provides a way for those who pray to respond to their growing relationship with God. It can also be a real blessing to the pastors, the recipients of the care visits, and even the whole church. The purpose of this ministry is to assist the pastor and leaders in meeting the pastoral care needs of the church. Lay participation in this area of ministry is desirable and necessary. Even in small churches where pastors alone are able to visit all the homebound and hospitalized, lay people should be involved because this ministry belongs to the whole body of Christ, not only to the clergy. The whole church should share this opportunity and responsibility. In addition, carrying out this ministry strengthens the care minister's, as well as the recipient's, relationship with God.

In some prayer care ministries, participants are asked to provide only support and prayer. Other pastoral care programs, such as Stephen Ministry, offer extensive training for ongoing, in-depth ministry. Pastoral care programs can be combined with prayer care ministries to strengthen both the pastoral care and prayer aspects of the ministries. Whether this is appropriate will depend on the church's size, resources, and understanding of its mission.

The key to the prayer care ministry is training for the care ministers. People might be reluctant to enter a hospital or someone's home to pray for and perhaps serve Communion to those who are hurting or alone. A strong training program, including a combination of theory and actual hands-on experience, can alleviate the fears and help caregivers feel confident about their ministry. Certainly, you want to recruit people who are mature in their Christian faith, people who understand and support the vision of the church and who are growing in their own prayer life.

A training manual (see Appendix D) could include information on
- the mission and goals of the program
- nurturing and caring for persons with special needs
- listening (the skill most critical for care ministers to learn)
- praying for and with others
- record keeping

If care ministers will be serving Holy Communion, they also should receive instruction on the theology of Holy Communion and the act of serving Communion.

The pastor or an experienced care minister should accompany care ministers on their first visits. The new care ministers can be introduced to the people they will be visiting, observe the visit, and later ask questions about the visit. After one or two such visits, the pastor or experienced care minister can primarily observe and evaluate the new ministers and help assess their readiness for the work. These companion visits also help ease the transition for the care recipient, who might be quite attached to the pastor or experienced care minister.

At the conclusion of the training, the prayer care minister should be officially recognized as a person set apart by the church for this ministry. At that time, a care ministry certification card can be given to all who complete the training. When the care minister goes to a hospital or other care facility, the card serves to introduce the person as a representative of the church.

Face to Face with God
CARE MINISTRY
This certifies that

_____

has completed the training to be a Joy Care Minister and is representing Community Church of Joy.

PRAYER CHAPEL

Intermediate Ministry

Synopsis   A room in or near the sanctuary is set aside for people who seek ministry through prayer following the worship service or at other designated times.

Resources Required   • A private room, in or near the church sanctuary, available before and immediately after worship services

Description   The presence of a prayer chapel gives the ministry a distinct identity and communicates to the church that prayer and prayer ministry are valued so highly by the church that prime space is set aside for this ministry. This is especially important for a new prayer ministry. Having a prayer room
  • provides a place where people know they can come and pray
  • provides a place for longer times of prayer, such as prayer vigils
  • generally makes it easier to schedule prayer activities in the church
  • provides a place where reports about answers to prayer can be made and posted

Typically, the prayer room has one or more kneelers, a cross, candles, some chairs, one or more boards for reporting answers to prayers, perhaps a map or two, and maybe some art. If the prayer room is used to pray for the sick, anointing oil may be required. Some prayer rooms have scheduled times when people can come and receive prayer for healing.

Depending on how it will be used, a prayer room can be any size. Some larger prayer rooms have prayer stations, separate places of prayer focusing on particular topics, such as confession, thanksgiving, pastor(s) and staff, the church, the community, the body of Christ, and the whole world. Each station can be identified with pictures, prayer lists, and related items that help direct attention to the prayer theme. For example, the station focusing on the pastor(s) and staff may have pictures of these people and their families, with lists of their names, birth dates, and activities.

There are some real advantages to organizing the prayer room in this manner. For example, it provides structured movement during prayer time, breaking up long periods of prayer and making them more interesting, especially for people new to the prayer room. A drawback is that prayer stations require a room of significant size. One strategy might be to start with a smaller room and pray that the ministry will grow and a larger room will become available.

A prayer chapel or prayer room can serve different functions.
  • It can be a quiet room where people can come at any time to pray. This room should be easy to get to and might even have its own entrance to the outside. In some churches, the prayer chapel is open night and day. Establishing such a room could be a start-up prayer ministry for a church.
  • In some instances, the prayer chapel or prayer room is located in or near the sanctuary and is used primarily by people seeking ministry through

prayer following Sunday morning worship services. Sunday morning worshipers are made aware of the prayer chapel through notes in the bulletin and announcements during the service. Those interested can come and pray, either alone or with a person trained to pray for and with others. The pastor might go to the prayer chapel after leading the service to pray with those who desire prayer. Or prayer team members can receive the people who come to the prayer chapel, pray for them, and suggest follow-up activities. A more detailed description of the development and workings of a prayer team is found on page 86.

- A prayer chapel can also be used by intercessors who come regularly to pray for a variety of concerns: staff and members of the church; family and friends of members; the neighborhood, community, the nation, or troubled parts of the world; people known to be sick or hospitalized; those who grieve; those who celebrate; and others. There is usually a sign-up sheet so intercessors can schedule time in the chapel. Some prayer rooms are always open. Others are available from early morning to night. For more information on a ministry of intercession, see page 88.

The prayer room can be expanded to include a prayer telephone ministry (see page 96), open prayer times, and many other activities. However, take care not to allow the prayer room to become an activity center, crowding out time for prayer. The prayer room is first and foremost a place to pray. Resist the temptation to use it for anything else.

APPENDIX C
ADVANCED MINISTRIES

PRAYER TEAM MINISTRY

Advanced Ministry

Synopsis

A team of trained persons meet in the prayer chapel before or after the worship service to pray with those who desire personal prayer.

Resources Required

- A team of people who feel called and are trained to pray on a team, and who are willing to commit to this ministry
- One or more persons to recruit, train, schedule, and coordinate prayer team members
- A brief training program
- A statement of confidentiality to be signed by all prayer team members (see page 51)
- Someone to receive, process, and update prayer requests
- Promotion about the opportunity to be prayed for
- A board on which to post reports about answers to prayers
- A quiet prayer room, available any time
- Money for training materials and supplies

Description

For an introduction to this idea, refer to the intermediate prayer ministry, Prayer Chapel, on page 82.

Developing a good prayer team ministry involves extensive training and a significant commitment by both trainers and team members. But it is an investment well worth the time and effort. People's lives are transformed by prayer and follow-up ministry.

Prayer team members need to be able to do three things:
- Listen well (to hear what people are really saying, but also to understand what God wants to do for the person seeking prayer support).
- Pray with sensitivity, confidence, and specificity.
- Be able to give post-prayer direction (to be able to answer the question, Where do I go from here?). In order to answer this question well, prayer team members must know what is available in the church and community for follow-up care. An excellent prayer team ministry follows up on what happens in the prayer chapel. Members see the prayer team ministry as a beginning point and know that God uses a variety of means to bring about healing, nurture, and growth.

Prayer team training needs to include:
- Instruction about biblical material on prayer; kinds of prayer, especially healing prayer; and listening
- Opportunities to pray
- Instruction on policies and procedures in the prayer chapel

(See Appendix D for material that could be included in a training program.)

A church with an established prayer team can design a mentor program that gives trainees opportunities to watch what is taking place in the prayer chapel, to pray jointly with an experienced prayer team member, and finally to pray alone as the mentor observes (and later offers helpful feedback). When the mentor and the trainee agree that training is complete, the person becomes a prayer team member. In churches without established prayer teams, a course can still be developed to provide theoretical training for future prayer team members. No matter how training is provided, it helps new prayer team members feel confident about the ministry they will be carrying out.

The prayer team ministry usually takes place in a room near the sanctuary where team members and people seeking prayer support can meet. In some churches the prayer team offers prayer in the front of the church or at the altar following the worship service. However, in most churches a private prayer chapel or room is desirable, especially if the church has back-to-back worship services or other activity in the sanctuary after worship.

If your church has more than one worship service, try to organize one prayer team for each service. The work load is better distributed that way, and burnout is significantly reduced.

MINISTRY *of* INTERCESSION
Advanced Ministry

Synopsis

This ministry provides local intercessors opportunities to pray for the needs of others.

Resources Required

- A team of people who feel called and are trained to offer intercessory prayer, and who are willing to commit to this ministry
- One or more persons to recruit, train, schedule, and coordinate intercessors
- A brief training program
- A statement of confidentiality to be signed by all participating intercessors
- Someone to receive, process, and update prayer requests
- A prayer list with updated prayer needs
- A board on which to post reports about answers to prayers
- A quiet prayer room, available any time
- Money for training materials and supplies

Description

Ministries of intercession can range from groups praying in homes for their church and community, to a worldwide ministry with computer and telephone equipment to receive, track, and send prayer requests. To develop a ministry of intercession for your church, it is important to be sensitive to God's direction, since there are many options to consider. A ministry of intercession will have significant impact on the life and ministry of the local church and far beyond.

Begin by seeking God's guidance about the shape and timing of the ministry, and ask for God's wisdom about who should lead the ministry. Then focus on these three items:

- Locate a prayer room. (Although it might not be practical to use the prayer chapel for this ministry, there are many similarities between the two types of rooms. See page 82 for a description of a prayer chapel, and use your best judgment about the intercession room's special needs).
- Select or develop a training program for the intercessors (see Appendix D).
- Recruit intercessors.

The heart of the ministry of intercession, once established, is lists of selected topics, identified needs, and prayer requests. These lists form the prayer guide and might be organized in a three-ring binder. Some lists and items, including the following, might remain in the guide all the time:

- Staff, members, friends, and ministries of the church
- Staff, ministries, and missions of your church's denomination
- The body of Christ throughout the world
- The global village
- God's whole creation

Other lists include requests received through the coordinator. For example, prayers might be requested for the sick or hospitalized, for those who grieve, for those who celebrate, and for other needs.

In the front of the guide, include detailed instructions about how it is organized and how to use it. There might be two sets of instructions: a detailed version for new intercessors and a summary version for experienced intercessors. A large bookmark can be left in the guide to indicate where the last intercessor stopped praying and the new intercessor should begin. You might want to devise a tracking system, so that all intercessors can leave a complete record of their involvement.

A separate sheet might provide an outline for the intercessor's prayer time. For example:

- Begin by quieting yourself and beginning to focus on God. Praise God in whatever manner suits you.
- Lay before God any concerns or needs you have that might interfere with your prayer. Confess any brokenness in your relationship with God, family or friends, yourself, or the rest of creation.
- Give thanks to God as you feel moved, especially for calling you to be a child of God, for calling you to this ministry, and for answering our prayers.
- Offer intercession for yourself and your family or friends, as they have need.
- Turn to the marker in the intercession guide and pray as God leads you for as many items as you have time for.
- Place the marker in the guide where you finished praying.
- Again thank God for hearing and answering our prayers.

Training for intercessors will be very similar to training for prayer team members (see page 86). Intercessors need to learn about prayer, to pray (perhaps with a mentor at first), and to understand procedures for the ministry.

HEALING PRAYER MINISTRY

Advanced Ministry

Synopsis

This ministry provides opportunities for people to seek healing prayer for illness in spirit, soul, and body.

Resources Required

For a monthly service for healing prayer:
- A person or several people to plan, promote, lead, and pray for healing during the service

For a more extensive ministry:
- An individual or small committee to plan and implement the ministry, and possibly to recruit and train people who feel called to pray for healing.
- A training manual or program, purchased or developed according to local needs and circumstances. (See Richard J. Beckmen, *Praying for Wholeness and Healing* [Minneapolis: Augsburg Fortress, 1995] or contact The International Order of St. Luke, P.O. Box 13701, San Antonio, TX 78213, 512/492-5222. See also Appendix D.)
- Money for training, if required.

Description

The prayer coordinator or committee needs to make recommendations about what form the ministry should take. Here are some suggestions.
- Small groups focus on studying and/or offering healing prayer.
- Classes about healing prayer are set up. These classes might also provide opportunities for participants to receive and/or practice healing prayer.
- Prayer teams pray for people individually in their homes, following regular worship services at church, or at other times and places.
- Open or corporate prayer meetings with an emphasis on healing are held.
- Services of Holy Communion include prayer for healing.

One possibility is to start with two healing prayer opportunities that complement each other:
- A class with primary focus on healing prayer
- A special healing service open to the entire church and others who might want to attend

The classes can serve as the training program for those who will pray for healing at the special healing services, and can also be open to anyone who wants to know more about healing prayer. If they are used for training, the classes need to include both the theory and the practice of praying for healing. For example, the instructor might talk about the biblical and historical roots of the practice of laying on of hands during healing prayer. And then the instructor can demonstrate the prayer and invite the class to pray in this manner.

The healing service itself can follow the liturgy or order of the regular worship service, or a specially designed service. Services can be scheduled in different ways, depending on what seems best for the church.

- Prayers for healing might be periodically incorporated into a regular worship service. Prayers for healing might be offered monthly, quarterly, or as suggested by the day's lessons or the church year (for example, when the Sunday lessons are about healing, or on or near October 18, the festival day of St. Luke).
- A new worship service might be introduced as a specific opportunity for healing prayer.

Some churches like variety in the healing prayer service. Others follow a set pattern that people become accustomed to. Here are some ideas.

- The pastor or the service leader prays for the church corporately, and people remain in their places.
- Worshipers form groups of three and four to pray for each other according to needs.
- People are invited to come to the altar or another designated spot to receive healing prayer from the pastor and/or members of the healing team.
- People are invited to come to the altar for Holy Communion and can receive healing prayer at the altar rail or move to a designated place—one side of the altar or a pew at the side of the sanctuary, for example.

Healing prayer services, at least from time to time, ought to include opportunities for people to talk about how God has answered prayers. Such stories are a great encouragement, especially to those who pray for healing.

If possible, before beginning your ministry talk to the pastor and members of another church with an established healing ministry. They can often provide valuable insights, help you avoid potential problems, and get you pointed in the right direction.

PRAYER PARTNERS MINISTRY

Advanced Ministry

Synopsis

Through this ministry, members of the church are enabled to pray for specific individuals locally, nationally, and/or internationally.

Resources Required

- A coordinator to organize the ministry
- Someone who will select prayer partners according to predetermined guidelines, either by hand or with a computer program
- Money and volunteers to prepare a mass mailing

Description

The prayer partners ministry offers many opportunities for prayer involvement. It is a relatively simple idea: put two people or families in contact with each other so they can pray for each other.

To see how the ministry works, the church could introduce the concept to the staff and the church council members and let them try it out for six months. (Starting small also has the advantage of letting coordinators work out the bugs before the numbers make things more difficult to manage.)

To begin, send a short letter to participants explaining how the ministry works. (See next page for a sample.) Participants are asked to do three things:

- Contact and introduce themselves to their assigned prayer partners.
- Invite the prayer partners to request prayer for two or three specific things, and then pray regularly for those requests.
- Periodically check back with the prayer partner to see how he or she is doing and to invite new prayer requests.

Each pair of partners can decide how to establish contact: by phone, letter, personal visit, fax, or even electronic mail. Participants can also decide for themselves how to pray, when, and how often. Most will probably address the prayer partner's prayer concerns during their regular prayer time.

It's important to formulate prayer partner guidelines. The guidelines might be as follows:

- Single men are matched with single men, single women with single women.
- Families are divided into three separate groups.
  - Nuclear families are matched with nuclear families.
  - Single men with children are matched with other single men with children.
  - Single women with children are matched with other single women with children.
- Children are asked to pray for their siblings or for their own families.

Not everyone invited participates in the partnership ministry. In that event, the partner who chooses to participate is still encouraged to pray for the partner who does not. The ministry should have a sunset provision that concludes the partnership after one, or in some instances, two years. At that time, all partnerships are rematched. Every effort should be made to find partners who want to participate actively for people who have had inactive partners during the previous year. People who join the church during the year can be matched with others who join at the same time or can simply wait until the next matching takes place.

A church's prayer partnership ministry can be expanded to establish prayer partnerships with other churches. For example, ten families might be motivated to pray for partners in another church. Some basic information and pictures can be exchanged. Otherwise, these prayer partnerships are very similar to the local ones. Yet another step is to invite international prayer partnerships with members of another church.

Dear Dwight, Kathy and Erin:

This is one of the most important letters you will ever receive from your church. You are a valuable part of our church's ministry. One way we can demonstrate how cherished you are is to pray for you. That is exactly what the pastors, staff, and leaders of our church do regularly.

Now we are inviting you to pray regularly for another member of our church. We are asking all our members to become a prayer partner to another member. During the coming year, we invite you to pray for the following people:

Jonathan, AnnMarie, and Rickey Olson
290 Hometown Way
Minneapolis, MN 55401
555-4444

Please contact the Olson family as soon as possible. Make a phone call, write a note, or talk in person, and simply ask, "What would you like me to pray for?" (If your partner(s) do not have a specific prayer request, simply pray for them to grow in their relationship with God.)

Then check in with your prayer partner periodically—about once a month. Ask whether the prayer has been answered and whether the person would like to have your prayers for another concern. If there are others in your household, invite them to pray for the partner(s), too.

Our prayer is that you will be richly blessed as you become a partner in this ministry.

Sincerely,

Pastor Mueller

INTERCESSORY SUPPORT MINISTRY

Advanced Ministry

Synopsis   A team of intercessors pray regularly at the request of a leader.

Resources Required

- Someone to identify and recruit intercessors for the support team
- Someone to train intercessors
- A way to communicate prayer concerns to the support team and someone to manage that communication

Description   Prayer support is important for all of us, and especially for leaders. The apostle Paul frequently says, "Pray also for me" (for example, see Ephesians 6:19). In 1 Timothy 2:1-2, Paul says, "First of all, then, I urge that supplications, prayers, intercession and thanksgivings be made for everyone, for kings and all who are in high positions."

More than ever, prayer support is of utmost importance. Leaders need to be undergirded with prayers. Our churches, communities, and nation need strong leaders, people of honesty, integrity, and deep devotion to Jesus Christ. Such leaders need to be supported with much prayer. An intercessory support ministry in a church, the ministry discussed here, provides a structure for prayer support for the church's pastor(s). Support intercessors are regularly informed about and pray for the leader's needs, issues, and priorities.[5]

There are several types of intercessors. Some intercessors have only casual contact or no contact with the pastor. An example is someone who reads about and decides to pray for a particular missionary or ministry. The intercessor might never meet the missionary or see the ministry in action but still feel a desire to pray for the person or work. This type of support intercessor might be someone from a previous church, a relative, or someone who senses a special call to pray for the church and its pastor. The person takes the initiative and indicates that he or she would like to pray for the pastor. The intercessor then usually receives a monthly or quarterly letter that includes a list of requests for prayer from the pastor. (The list is prepared by or under the direction of the pastor.)

Some intercessors are recruited by the pastor. These people usually know the pastor and communicate with him or her as often as the pastor has requests, perhaps monthly or even weekly. These intercessors are people of prayer and might be discovered quite simply: they typically shake the pastor's hand at the end of the worship service and say, "Pastor, I pray for you." People involved in other prayer ministries of the church are also excellent candidates for this special intercession.

Finally, a support intercessor might be a person with whom the pastor has considerable contact, perhaps weekly face-to-face or telephone contact. This person is very sensitive to the Holy Spirit's guidance and has gifts to discern God's leading. This primary intercessor is not recruited but is brought to the leader through prayer, and leaders should not be in a hurry to find one. This type of intercessor is a rare gift, one that all who pray for a leader will want to ask God to raise up.

To help the support intercessors work well, the leader needs to
- maintain regular and frequent communication
- listen to what the intercessors are saying
- find ways to recognize the intercessors and let them know how much they are appreciated
- pray regularly for the intercessors and their families

Leaders should also remember these helpful tips:
- Watch out for intercessors who try to control the leader by saying things like, "God says you must … ." God speaks to all God's children, including leaders. Leaders need to listen but also to weigh all sources of information and communication. It is good to be cautious, especially with new and inexperienced intercessors who mean well but are still learning.
- The leader and primary intercessor, who will be in frequent contact, probably should be of the same sex. This can be difficult for male leaders because so many intercessors are women. A male leader can take a few men under his wing, mentoring them and helping them grow in their prayer relationship with God and in the ministry of intercessory prayer.
- It is not necessary to have many intercessory supporters to make a difference. One or two people praying for a leader regularly will have a significant impact. Relying on a small team has some advantages: communication is easier, more personal contact can be maintained, training is easier, and the leader can grow with the team.

PRAYER TELEPHONE MINISTRY

Advanced Ministry

Synopsis

This ministry allows people to receive prayer inspiration and/or support by telephone.

Resources Required

Depending on the complexity of the ministry:
- A coordinator
- A telephone with a dedicated, well-publicized number
- Volunteers to staff the phone
- A trainer and training program for the volunteers
- A referral system for emergencies
- A separate room where calls can be received and attended to
- Money

Description

Prayer telephone ministries vary considerably. Perhaps the simplest system is a dial-a-prayer ministry, in which the caller hears a recorded message and prayer. The taped message might include a scripture verse or two, a brief inspirational message, and a prayer. This ministry might be seen as the first step toward establishing a more complex ministry, or it might be in itself the ministry the church is called to.

A slightly more complex ministry is to invite callers to record prayer requests following the recorded message. Then it becomes necessary to catalog the requests and make sure each is offered in prayer by an intercessor.

Some ministries go one step further and ask the people who request prayer to identify themselves and leave their telephone numbers for follow-up contact. This adds significantly to the resource requirements of the ministry. One or more prayer counselors are needed to contact each person who has requested prayer attention. All requests need to be addressed fairly promptly or the ministry will lose effectiveness and even credibility.

One type of prayer telephone ministry focuses on three areas:
- Listening to the caller's concerns
- Praying with the caller
- Referring the caller for follow-up care, if needed

The emphasis in this ministry is on listening, prayer, and referral, rather than counseling. Of course, volunteers need some diagnostic skills so they can refer callers to the appropriate person or organization. But it is clear to callers and telephone volunteers that this telephone ministry is a prayer service, not a counseling session.

In the most complex prayer telephone ministry, people answer the phone during designated hours or even around the clock. Developing this kind of ministry is a major undertaking, of course. In some communities, several churches form a joint telephone ministry, perhaps forming a separate organization to accomplish their goals. In other communities, a large church or several churches might form a working relationship with a Christian or community counseling service or hospital emergency hot line to provide a live answering service for people seeking spiritual and emotional support.

To develop this most complex type of prayer telephone ministry in the church, the designated room needs to have comfortable chairs, a good-sized work station for the prayer counselor, and appropriate resource materials. Essential resources are a telephone with features such as call forwarding, notification of a second incoming call, voice mail, and so on; a Bible with a list of verses appropriate for a wide variety of spiritual and emotional challenges; a directory of community mental health and emergency services; and a manual of guidelines for handling especially difficult situations. A form (perhaps on computer) for making notes about the situation and recommended follow-up needs to be developed. If no computer is available, a filing system of some kind should be designed.

If a church decides to offer a more extensive ministry, the prayer counselors need special training. Some training programs last as long as a year or two. Prayer counselors for this type of ministry should have an excellent background in counseling, emergency care, spiritual guidance, and prayer, and be well equipped to address almost any situation. Ironically, the strength of this approach can also be a major challenge, since it might be hard to get people to commit to such extensive training.

To determine what kind of prayer telephone ministry is best for your church, ask for God's guidance and direction. Then consider the following:

- Need for such a prayer telephone ministry
- Availability of prayer telephone ministries in the area
- Availability of hot lines in the area
- Availability of referral services
- Church's resources
- Availability of intercessors who can provide prayer support for the ministry and participate in the telephone ministry

CONCERT *of* PRAYER

Advanced Ministry

Synopsis

Christians from many different churches and denominations gather to enjoy fellowship, to worship, and especially to pray together.

Resources Required

- An interdenominational committee to plan, organize, and implement the event.
- Money to promote the concert, print up programs, and, if necessary, rent an appropriate facility. Depending on the number of people expected to participate, a larger facility such as an auditorium might need to be leased. (Some or all of the expenses might be covered by a freewill offering, although money might still be needed for deposits.)
- In larger communities, well-known outside speakers are brought in to participate or lead the concert of prayer. They can help draw more people into the event, but their assistance costs more money.
- Musicians.

Description

Concerts of prayer are growing in popularity. They can be organized within one church but typically involve many churches from various denominations. Obviously, a concert of prayer can be a major undertaking, even for several churches. Cooperation and good working relationships are important both for effective organization and for broad support during the event itself.

Early planning allows churches to get the event on their calendars, allows plenty of time for renting the facility and securing one or more speakers, and increases opportunities for promoting the event. Keep in mind that the more well known the speaker, the earlier he or she needs to be contacted.

During the concert of prayer, worship and prayer—especially prayer—are the main activities. One of the special features of such an event is that it affords opportunities for different kinds of prayer. The event might include

- individual silent prayer
- corporate prayer
- prayer triplets (three people praying together)
- prayer huddles (three groups of triplets praying together)
- prayer through worship and praise

The concert is usually about two hours long. Each segment may be introduced by a different leader, allowing many people the opportunity to be involved as leaders for the concert, promoting unity and harmony in the local church community, and encouraging participation by more churches.

David Bryant, the international director of Concerts of Prayer, Inc., suggests the following format for a concert of prayer:[6]

- **Celebration** (15 minutes)
  - Praise with music that focuses on awakening and mission
  - Reports of God's answers to prayers offered during previous concerts

- Prayers of praise for God's love and faithfulness and God's many gifts to us
- **Preparation** (20 minutes)
  - Welcome to the concert
  - Overview: Why we are here
  - Biblical perspective on what we're praying for (for example, the spread of the gospel, our future as a nation)
  - Preview of the format
  - Praying in triplets and huddles
- **Prayer of dedication** (5 minutes)
  - Commitment to be God's servants through prayer and to be God's instruments for answering prayer
  - Thanks for the privilege of uniting in prayer and for those with whom we pray
  - Petition for the Holy Spirit to lead the concert and to pray through us
- **Seeking growth in our relationship with God and awakening in the church** (30 minutes)
  - Praying in triplets for personal growth
  - Praying in huddles for awakening in our local churches and ministries
  - Praying as a whole for awakening in the church worldwide
  - Pause to listen to God
  - Special music, hymn, or song
- **Seeking fulfillment of the Great Commission among all people** (30 minutes)
  - Praying in triplets for personal ministries
  - Praying in huddles for outreach and mission in our city or community
  - Praying as a whole for all who do not know God
  - Pause to listen to God
  - Special music, hymn, or song
- **Reflection: What has God said here?** (10 minutes)
  - On the growth of Christians' relationships with God (awakening)
  - On fulfillment of the Great Commission (mission)
- **Closing** (10 minutes)
  - Offering ourselves to be instruments of the answers to our prayers
  - Praying for God to empower us for ministry
  - Praying for people everywhere to discover the power of prayer
  - Offering praise to God, who answers prayer
  - Leaving to serve "in concert"

SCHOOL *or* COLLEGE *of* PRAYER

Advanced Ministry

Synopsis

This ministry offers courses about various aspects of prayer to encourage individual growth and development of leaders for specific prayer ministries.

Resources Required

The complexity of the school or college determines to a large degree the resources required. Basic needs include:

- A coordinator for the school's planning and implementation
- A task force or committee to address such issues as goals, instructors, curriculum selection and development, budget requirements, promotion, future direction, and so on
- Money, depending on how you decide to pay for materials and other needs
- If possible, someone from a church with a school of prayer to consult

Description

A school or college of prayer is primarily for larger churches, although the ministry can be developed on a small scale or with other churches in the area. In addition to prayers for guidance and effectiveness, a school needs

- an excellent curriculum
- knowledgeable, faithful, and compassionate instructors
- a promotion plan that will bring new students into the ministry

Curriculum needs to be compatible with your church's theology and traditions. But it also must suit the needs of the students. If possible, provide courses suitable for several levels of experience and commitment. Assume that inexperienced pray-ers will always be entering the ministry, so design at least one introductory course that will not discourage or overwhelm them. Also assume that after they have taken several introductory courses, students will be looking for something more. Design courses to challenge them appropriately. On every level, it is probably better to offer several shorter courses, rather than one long one.

Finally, remember that prayer always leads to action. Courses on every level should provide opportunities for people to become involved in an activity. Beginners might make a commitment to offer prayers of intercession for the items suggested on the church prayer calendar. Someone with more experience might decide to become part of a prayer team and call on a homebound member or friend of the church to offer basic pastoral care. The most experienced students might become leaders or trainers for various prayer ministries in the church.

Of course, pray-ers at all levels might also choose to move from prayer to action in the community or beyond. Offering intercession for people or even nations in need, volunteering for a community tutoring program, or taking vacation time to help with a Habitat for Humanity project are all actions that might grow out of a person's prayer.

Courses can be selected and developed in the following ways:
- Use existing materials from outside sources.
- Take an existing resource, such as a good book on prayer, and develop a course based on it. If you begin with an audiocassette or video, you might want to develop a study guide to go with it.
- Create new curriculum. Obviously, this is more time consuming and challenging, but it might be the best way to meet your church's individual needs.

Prayer has many expressions. One way to develop courses is to look at various prayers. For example:
- General prayer
- Intercessory prayer
- Healing prayer
- Listening or meditative prayer
- Prayer journaling
- Praying and fasting
- Worship and praise

Another idea is to develop short courses on specific areas of need. Here are several examples, some of which could be combined:
- Devotional prayer
- Praying for and with children
- Praying in tough times
- Prayer and forgiveness
- Praying with the sick
- Praying for leaders
- Prayer and evangelism
- Prayer ministry training

A recognition service is a great opportunity both to recognize achievement and create interest among potential students. For greatest impact, the recognition or graduation might be incorporated into a Sunday morning worship service.

HOUSE *of* PRAYER

Advanced Ministry

Synopsis

A home or other building is dedicated to prayer, especially intercession for the surrounding neighborhood.

Resources Required

- A home or other building
- At least one person, possibly someone living in the house, who is willing to coordinate prayer activities and be available for discussion and prayer
- Strong prayer support from outside intercessors
- Means of communicating to others the purpose and mission of the house of prayer
- Money, depending on the kind of facility chosen

Description

A house of prayer can be a home where regularly scheduled prayer meetings are open for anyone to attend. Some are special places where intercessory prayer is offered on a regular basis. It is unlikely that a small church would start a house of prayer in which lengthy intercessory prayer is offered. However, smaller churches, communities, or denominations might pool their resources to develop a house of prayer ministry. Larger churches might have more resources and be better able to launch such a project themselves.

Houses of prayer place a sign in the window or some other strategic place, inviting the neighbors to come there to pray individually or with others in prayer meetings. Ministry participants may also walk from door to door and ask neighbors if they have any concerns for which they would like prayer. Such visits may include an invitation to come to the house to pray or to attend a prayer meeting. Visitors might leave behind a brochure explaining the purpose of the house of prayer and letting neighbors know it is available for their prayer needs.

A list of the neighbors and their prayer needs can be developed, and then intercessors can offer prayers for these needs, along with prayer for other concerns.

APPENDIX D
TRAINING INTERCESSORS

This appendix outlines a suggested process for training people who would like to offer intercessory prayer face-to-face with people in need. The training can be adapted for a variety of ministries, including prayer care ministry, prayer team ministry, ministry of intercession, and healing prayer ministry. Material in this guide provides the core for about four hours of training, assuming that the trainer will begin with devotions; include time for questions, discussion, and practicing the topics being presented; and schedule appropriate breaks. Training may be conducted in one half-day or two, two-hour sessions.

The trainer should be aware of participants' experience with intercessory prayer.

As each person is invited to join a ministry of intercession, he or she should be asked to fill out a survey like the one on the last page of this appendix. The information on the survey will be useful for basic record keeping and, more important, will help the trainer shape sessions to meet the needs of the participants.

To the Session Leader: Begin the training session with a brief welcome and prayer. Ask group members to introduce themselves to the other group members and to describe briefly what made them decide to participate in this training. Outline the schedule for the training sessions.

Part I: The Prayer Session

Key aspects of this ministry

The three key aspects of a ministry of intercession are
- listening to God and finding out what God wants to do through our prayers
- listening to the person who requests prayers and finding out what his or her needs are
- under the guidance of the Holy Spirit, ministering to the person in need

This ministry includes encouragement, various forms of prayer, and postprayer direction (sometimes including referral for other types of help).

Prayer partners

Often intercessors will pray with a partner. One of the team members will be more active, asking questions, clarifying needs, and praying out loud. The other partner will act as the "compassionate observer," watching the person's face and body language and asking God to help discern what unspoken needs the person might have. (If the intercessor prays alone, he or she will have to tend to both these tasks as well as possible.) The active partner begins the conversation while the compassionate observer focuses on listening to the person and to God, and discerning what is needed and what God is directing.

Step One: Interview the person to be prayed for.

The intercessors approach the person in love. The active partner asks, "Would you like someone to pray for you?" Both intercessors introduce themselves, using first names only. The active partner asks, "What is your name?" (It is important that both intercessors remember the person's name.)

The active partner then asks, "What prayer would you like me to offer for you?" The active intercessor might need to help the person put into words what the concern is. Open-ended questions are usually helpful. (Ask, for example, "Could you say more about that?") The intercessor might also feed back in his or her own words what the person said. Such feedback gives the person an opportunity to clarify or correct statements and often prompts the person to continue talking.

Both intercessors listen! The compassionate observer especially watches the person's facial expressions and posture and listens to the person's tone of voice and speech patterns. The observer also prays silently for God's guidance and for clarity about the person's root problem. If the observer intercessor notices signs that there is an issue that should be explored further or anything else that might affect the prayer, he or she might gently ask another question or make a suggestion to the active partner about how to proceed. Throughout their time together, the intercessors should be careful not to alarm the person with information or insights the person might not want to receive.

The active partner decides how to pray for the person in need, remembering that the Holy Spirit prays through us when we do not know how to pray. Of course, the decision about how to pray takes into account both the needs of the person being prayed for and the promptings of the Spirit. Will the prayer be one of thanksgiving or encouragement, or for healing, inner peace, or wisdom? Should the prayer be out loud or silent? Will the intercessor alone pray, or will the person who is making the request pray? Will the intercessor offer a prayer and ask the person to repeat it? Should the intercessors use laying on of hands or anoint with oil?

Step Two: Decide how to pray.

The active partner prays for the concerns expressed, to the best of his or her recollection. The pray-er might mention that God has commanded us to pray and has promised to answer our prayers, and that God is present as we are praying. Sometimes the intercessor will be led to pray specifically: "Lord, heal Bob's headache," rather than simply, "Lord, heal Bob." Other times the intercessor will offer a more open-ended prayer, perhaps even asking for direction from the Holy Spirit: "Lord, we do not know how to pray in this situation, but we come to you with open hands, ready to receive whatever gifts you bring."

Step Three: Offer the prayer.

If it seems appropriate, one or both intercessors might touch the person being prayed for. Laying on hands is not an empty gesture. We read in Mark 6:5 and Luke 4:40 that Jesus laid on hands when he prayed for healing. In Acts 8:17, the people of Samaria received the Holy Spirit when Peter and John laid hands on them and prayed. And when Jesus blessed the children in Mark 10:16, he laid hands on them. If the person being prayed for seems receptive (if in doubt, ask) and the intercessors feel moved to do so, they might gently but firmly place their hands on the person's head or shoulder.

The prayer need not be long. Sometimes we seem to think that the longer we pray, the more likely God will answer. But when he prayed for the leper in Matthew 8:2-3, Jesus simply said, "Be made clean!" There is a place for what is called "soaking prayer," when several people offer extended prayer for an individual. But such prayer is not required for every situation. Let God's Spirit provide direction.

After the active intercessor is finished praying, he or she may ask, "How do you feel?" If the compassionate observer has noticed anything, such as a change of expression or posture, a sense of warmth, tingling sensations, or a sense of peace, the observer should mention these things as possible signs of God's work. Remember, however, that God does not always answer our prayers immediately. Often we need to pray frequently over a long period of time. If nothing has happened, that is perfectly all right. The active intercessor should assure the person that God is at work in us and that the answer to our prayers may come in surprising ways. In fact, we should expect the unexpected when we pray.

Step Four: Assess the result.

Step Five: Give postprayer direction.

Although the purpose of this time together is to pray, not to counsel, the person just prayed for probably wonders what to do next. At times, little direction will be required, but this conversation can be crucial. At the very least, the intercessors should encourage the person and suggest that the person offer thanks for the ministry he or she has received. The intercessors might also suggest that the person continue to pray by using prayers similar to those just offered, or that the person seek out the company of other Christians in worship and other settings.

Sometimes more specific direction is needed. For example:

- See a doctor for medical advice.
- See a pastor or other Christian leader for spiritual direction. (If possible, the intercessors should make a specific suggestion.)
- Talk to a counselor or therapist. (Most pastors have developed a list of trusted people to whom they refer. Intercessors should have access to such a list.)
- Join a small group for support. (Again, if possible, a specific suggestion is best.)
- Return for further prayer at a specific time (by appointment, at the next scheduled prayer service, or at some other time).

Often the intercessor will suggest that the person read several scripture passages or a tract or short book (depending on what is needed and what the person seems open to) to receive further direction or comfort. A reproducible list of scripture references that might be helpful to intercessors is provided on page 111.

Part II: Common Prayer Requests

To the Session Leader: If the training is being conducted at a single event, give participants a break at this point.

Intercessors will encounter many kinds of needs when they meet with someone to offer prayer, but most requests will fall into one of the following areas.

A broken relationship with God

Whether or not a person talks about this issue, an intercessor will want to be attentive to any signs that the person's relationship with God is broken. Sometimes people who request prayer will say they have doubts about their relationship with God, the need and request will be clear and straightforward, and the intercessor may simply proceed. But sometimes what the person needs and what the person requests will not be the same. For example, when a person talks about not being sure he or she is saved or wanting to be closer to God, the intercessor should be aware that there might be other issues, such as guilt or anger, that need to be dealt with before the relationship with God will "feel right." Conversely, when a person talks about deep loneliness or lack of direction, the underlying issue might be the relationship with God.

When a person begins by speaking about his or her relationship with God, the intercessor will want to try to discern whether the root problem is the doubt itself or an underlying issue, such as deep-seated anger or resentment, or guilt about past behavior. If there seems to be another underlying problem, the intercessor might through gentle questioning and directing invite the person to address that root problem.

Another person might want to pray about a particular problem, on the other hand, when his or her faith is itself the issue. The person might not be a Christian or might have moved away from God for a number of years. The intercessor will want to be especially sensitive when praying with such a person, offering comfort and God's hospitality, and avoiding shaming or subtly scolding the person in need. If the person seems reluctant to explore his or her relationship with God, the intercessors should not pursue the matter. Simply continue with the indicated prayer request. At the end of the prayer time, the intercessor can extend an invitation to talk again another time if the person decides to explore the faith issue.

If the person is not a Christian or has been far from God for a long time and seems interested in learning more about the faith, the intercessor may offer assurance that God loves all of us and wants to welcome all people into the household of faith. Bible passages such as John 3:16 and 1 John 4:4, 9-10, and 13-18 may be helpful. The intercessor may then pray that the Holy Spirit will call the person into a relationship (or deeper relationship) with God. If the person feels moved to offer a prayer, the intercessor should be encouraging. The intercessor will certainly want to provide postprayer direction that will nurture the person's budding faith: encourage him or her to talk with a pastor, to attend a Bible class, or to attend a small group for faith explorers.

Healing

Jesus' ministry was a ministry of preaching, teaching, and healing. Many Christians take seriously the preaching and teaching ministries but think that healing was only for Jesus or only for his day. The church, however, has always been about healing, in some manner. In James 5:14-15 we read:

Are any among you sick? They should call for the elders of the church and have them pray over them, anointing them with oil in the name of the Lord. The prayer of faith will save the sick, …

There is much to learn about the ministry of healing, and those who feel called to such a ministry should probably receive more intensive training than can be offered in this session. (See *Praying for Wholeness and Healing* by Richard J. Beckmen [Minneapolis: Augsburg Fortress, 1995] for a valuable resource.) But anyone involved in a ministry of intercessory prayer will receive requests for prayers for healing.

Intercessors should remember that we are only channels of God's grace; God does the healing. That means that we can let go of the results. Those involved in healing ministry often distinguish between "cure" and "healing," and they find that even people who are not cured are healed (or blessed) in some way.

The intercessors may begin by simply asking, "What do you want God to do for you?" If a person requests prayer for healing but is not clear about what is needed, the intercessors might ask gentle, probing questions to help focus on a particular need. Especially if the person asks for healing prayer regarding spiritual or emotional matters, the intercessors might find that there is a difference between what is requested and the actual need, as mentioned above.

When the intercessors are ready to pray, they may hold the person's hand or lay hands on the affected area (if appropriate) or on the person's head or shoulder. Anointing with oil is usually appropriate, too. The intercessors might first show the person the oil and explain that it is a symbol of the Holy Spirit and an outward sign of the healing that God will bring. Of course, if the person seems reluctant to be anointed, the intercessors should refrain from doing so.

The intercessors proceed with prayer as God leads, sometimes asking for specific results and sometimes simply laying the need before God and remaining open to whatever healing God might bring. The prayer should end with thanks for God's love and compassion. Postprayer direction should include instruction about being open to possibilities (prayer for a deep emotional wound might result in healing of a physical ailment, for example), continuing prayer for healing alone and with others, and reading appropriate scripture. If the prayer was for physical healing, the person should also be encouraged to follow his or her doctor's orders until the doctor indicates that medical treatment is not needed. Finally, intercessors should encourage the person to report what the results of the prayer are.

Guilt

If a person has done something wrong and feels appropriate guilt about the matter, the prayer might be that the person will have the courage he or she needs to take action to make amends for the deed. The intercessors should encourage the person to return after taking action, and then prayers of absolution and thanksgiving may be offered.

Sometimes people continue to hang on to guilt, even after they have done all they can to atone for their actions. In these cases, the intercessors should offer assurance that God forgives us. 1 John 1:9 says, "If we confess our sins, he who is faithful and just will forgive our sins and cleanse us from all unrighteousness." The intercessor may pronounce absolution in the name of Jesus.

Sometimes a person feels guilt about a matter for which he or she was not responsible. People who were physically or sexually abused as children or teenagers often feel guilty, although they were the victims and not the perpetrators of the behavior. The intercessors should ask questions, listen attentively, and be as supportive and encouraging as possible. They then may offer whatever prayer seems appropriate at the time; for example, that the person will have the courage to seek professional help, experience relief from troublesome physical or emotional symptoms, be able to let go of deep anger and forgive the perpetrator, and so forth. The intercessor will also want to provide assurance that the person is not alone, that God is present, as are members of the Christian community. Abuse situations are usually quite complex, and as part of the postprayer direction, the intercessor will probably want to suggest that the person seek a therapist skilled in working with victims of abuse.

Anger

Because of our society's norms about anger, many people (especially women) have difficulty expressing anger. The intercessors probably will want to offer prayer that the person will be able to talk about the anger with God or another person. Skilled intercessors might even actually coach the person through such self-disclosure. If appropriate, the intercessor might pray that the person will be able to forgive someone who wronged him or her, or that the person will be able to let go of the anger. This intercessor also should be attentive to the possibility that the person needs to be directed to a counselor or pastor for extended discussion or therapy.

Depression is more than feeling "blue" or "down in the dumps." Depression, the manifestation of a neuro-chemical imbalance in the brain, is an illness that can have devastating results if left untreated. It may evolve over a period of time, or traumatic events, such as a significant loss or negative experience, might bring on depression quickly. On an emotional level, depression is often related to unresolved resentment, bitterness, or anger, feelings that a person turns in on himself or herself.

Depression

Typical symptoms of depression that intercessors should listen for or ask about include the following:
- significant decrease in normal human drives
- dramatic decrease or increase in appetite
- insomnia or excessive sleep
- chronic fatigue
- lack of interest in daily activities or a sense that activities are a burden
- withdrawal from normal activities
- lack of a sense of satisfaction or happiness
- difficulty concentrating
- feelings of worthlessness, guilt, or anger toward self
- thoughts about suicide or attempted suicide

If a person has three or more of these symptoms and they have lasted more than two weeks, the intercessor should encourage the person to seek professional help as soon as possible.

Intercessors can be helpful to those who suffer from depression. First, they can offer the person assurance that God is always with us, so we do not need to bear our burdens alone. God will never abandon us. God can heal us and wants us to come in prayer and ask for help in times of need. The psalmist writes, "The Lord is a stronghold for the oppressed, a stronghold in times of trouble" (Psalm 9:9). And Paul writes that nothing can separate us from the love of God (Romans 8:37-39).

Intercessors might discern whether the person needs to forgive someone toward whom he or she holds great resentment, bitterness, or anger. If the person harbors such feelings, the intercessor may pray for the person to be able to forgive the one who harmed him or her. The intercessor may also help the person begin to forgive. The person might be encouraged to pray simply, "Dear God, I don't know how to forgive _____. Show me the way." Or the person might "practice" forgiveness by saying, "I forgive _____ for _____."

The intercessors' postprayer direction may also be helpful for those who suffer from depression. The intercessor may suggest as many of the following strategies as seem helpful:
- Talk. Share your feelings with a close friend.
- Exercise. Take a brisk walk, ride a bike, or run for at least twenty minutes three times a week.
- Eat properly. A poor diet can worsen the symptoms of depression.
- Reduce or cut out consumption of caffeine and alcohol. Again, these substances tend to increase feelings of depression.
- Become involved in some activity. Doing something you enjoy can help lift your mood.
- Go to a funny movie. Laughter is therapeutic and can help put things in perspective.

- Think positively. Avoid negative or distorted thought patterns, putting yourself down, or thinking your problems are insurmountable.
- Use prescription medicine as directed by your doctor or psychiatrist.
- Seek counseling. Even people who are on medication should be talking to a professional counselor or therapist on a regular basis. If the counselor is not a Christian or someone with whom you feel comfortable discussing faith issues related to your depression, you might also seek support from a pastor, small group, or other mature Christian.

Anxiety

The intercessors invite the person to release his or her burdens to God and pray for peace for the person. John 14:27 might be helpful: "Peace I leave with you; my peace I give to you. I do not give to you as the world gives. Do not let your hearts be troubled, and do not let them be afraid."

Intercessors should also be aware that as with guilt, some anxiety is rooted in a person's own actions, and the person will need to change particular behavior or make amends for past behavior in order for the anxiety to leave.

Wisdom or direction

In James 1:5 we read, "If any of you is lacking in wisdom, ask God, who gives to all generously and ungrudgingly, and it will be given you." The intercessors can recall this promise and encourage the person to claim it for himself or herself.

Thanksgiving

Yes, sometimes people will ask for prayer to celebrate some good thing that has happened. And the apostle Paul tells us, "Rejoice with those who rejoice … ." So intercessors may simply enjoy themselves and rejoice with those who give thanks.

Conclusion

Once this basic training is completed, the new intercessor should be paired with an experienced, mature intercessor, who serves as a mentor. At first, the mentor will be the active partner and the trainee can serve as the compassionate observer during prayer. After prayer sessions, the mentor and trainee should take time to discuss what happened during the prayer. The trainee can ask questions, and the mentor can provide instruction. When the trainee seems ready, he or she may become the active intercessor while the mentor serves as the compassionate observer. Again, the two should meet for discussion after prayer sessions. When both intercessors agree the newcomer is ready to take an active role in the selected ministry, the trainee may be released to that ministry.

Organizational needs will depend on the particular ministry but will probably include provision for scheduling prayer times, ongoing discussion and training, and possibly a system for making referrals and keeping records. As appropriate, this initial training may include introduction of these administrative matters. Toward the end of the training session, it would be appropriate to give participants an evaluation form, so they can give feedback for improving future training sessions. And of course the session should end with a time of prayer.

SCRIPTURE REFERENCES *for* POST-PRAYER DIRECTION

Faith and Confidence

> Psalm 31:24
> Habakkuk 3:17-18
> Matthew 5:6
> John 15:7
> 2 Corinthians 5:7
> 2 Corinthians 9:8
> Philippians 4:13
> Hebrews 11:1

Comfort and Security

> Isaiah 26:3
> Isaiah 41:13
> John 14:1
> 1 Corinthians 10:13

Hope in Despair

> Psalm 42:5
> Romans 8:28
> Hebrews 12:11-12
> 1 Peter 5:7

Overcoming Anxiety

> Philippians 4:6-7
> 2 Timothy 1:7
> Hebrews 13:6

Overcoming Guilt

> Isaiah 43:25
> Romans 5:1
> 1 John 1:9

Guidance

> Proverbs 3:5-6
> Isaiah 30:21

Self-discipline

> Psalm 141:3
> Proverbs 16:32
> 1 Corinthians 13:4-5
> Philippians 4:8-9
> James 1:19-20

Life in Christ

> Matthew 6:33
> Matthew 16:25
> Galatians 2:20

Face to Face with God

MINISTRY *of* INTERCESSION
PARTICIPANT SURVEY

Name _____

Address _____

_____

_____

Daytime phone _____ Evening phone _____

1. How long have you been a Christian? _____

2. Are you a member of this church? ☐ Yes ☐ No

3. How long have you been a member of this church? _____

4. Have you ever prayed out loud for others or in a group? ☐ Yes ☐ No

    If yes, what was the setting or situation?

    _____

    _____

5. Are you comfortable praying out loud for others? ☐ Yes ☐ No

6. Have you received any training in praying for others, especially in praying for healing?
    ☐ Yes ☐ No

    If yes, please describe the type of training, and when and where you received it.

    _____

7. What would you most like to learn in these training sessions?

    _____

    _____

    _____

    _____

APPENDIX E
FOR FURTHER READING

FOR FURTHER READING

Beginning Conversations with God

Anonymous. *The Cloud of Unknowing.* New York: Image Books, 1973.

Bloom, Anthony. *Beginning to Pray.* New York: Paulist Press, 1979.

Brother Lawrence. *The Practice of the Presence of God.* Old Tappen, NJ: Revell, 1958.

Egan, Harvey D. *Christian Mysticism.* New York: Pueblo, 1984.

Foster, Richard J. *Prayer.* San Francisco: Harper, 1992.

Hallesby, O. *Prayer.* Minneapolis: Augsburg Fortress, 1993 (1931).

Kelsey, Morton T. *The Other Side of Silence.* New York: Paulist Press, 1976.

Klug, Ron. *How to Keep a Spiritual Journal.* Augsburg Fortress, 1994.

Michael, Chester D., and Marie C. Norrisey. *Prayer and Temperament.* Charlottesville, Va.: The Open Door Inc., 1984.

Pennington, M. Basil. *Centering Prayer.* New York: Image Books, 1980.

Sager, Allan H. *Gospel-Centered Spirituality.* Minneapolis: Augsburg Fortress, 1990.

Teresa of Avila. *The Interior Castle.* New York: Paulist Press, 1979.

Praying for Friends and Enemies

Barry, William A., S.J. *God and You: Prayer As Personal Relationship.* New York, Paulist Press, 1987.

Brueggemann, Walter. *The Message of the Psalms.* Minneapolis: Augsburg Publishing House, 1984.

Dossey, Larry, M.D. *Healing Words.* San Francisco: Harper San Francisco, 1993.

Froehle, Virginia Ann, R.S.M. *Called Into Her Presence: Praying with Feminine Images of God.* Notre Dame: Ave Maria Press, 1986.

Hall, Thelma, r.c. *Too Deep for Words: Rediscovering Lectio Divina.* New York: Paulist Press, 1988.

Huffmann, Walter C. *Prayer of the Faithful: Understanding and Creatively Leading Corporate Intercessory Prayer.* Minneapolis: Augsburg Fortress, 1992.

Keating, Thomas. *Intimacy With God.* New York: Crossroad, 1994.

Kushner, Harold S. *When Bad Things Happen to Good People.* New York: Schocken Books, 1981.

Leech, Kenneth. *True Prayer.* San Francisco: Harper and Row, Publishers, 1980.

Mollenkott, Virginia Ramey. *Godding: Human Responsibility and the Bible.* New York: Crossroad, 1987.

Moore, Thomas. *Care of the Soul.* New York: Harper Collins Publishers, 1992.

Nouwen, Henri J. M. *Reaching Out: The Three Movements of the Spiritual Life.* Garden City, New York: Doubleday and Company, Inc., 1975.

Rupp, Joyce, O.S.M. *Praying Our Goodbyes.* Notre Dame: Ave Maria Press, 1988.

Wiederkehr, Macrina. *A Tree Full of Angels: Seeing the Holy in the Ordinary.* San Francisco: Harper San Francisco, 1988.

Wink, Walter. *Engaging the Powers.* Minneapolis: Fortress Press, 1992.

Wuellner, Flora Slosson, *Prayer, Stress, and Our Inner Wounds.* Nashville: The Upper Room, 1985.

Praying for Wholeness and Healing

Darling, Frank C. *Biblical Healing: Hebrew and Christian Roots.* Boulder, CO: Vista Publications, 1989.

Darling, Frank C. *Christian Healing in the Middle Ages and Beyond.* Boulder, CO: Vista Publications, 1990.

Dossey, Larry, M.D. *Healing Words: The Power of Prayer and The Practice of Medicine.* New York: Harper San Francisco, 1993.

Glennon Jim. *Your Healing Is Within You: A Pastoral and Scriptural Presentation of the Healing Ministry of the Church.* South Plainfield, NJ: Bridge Pub., Inc. 1980.

Linn, Dennis & Matthew Linn. *Healing Life's Hurts: Healing Memories through the Five Stages of Forgiveness.* New York: Paulist Press, 1978.

MacNutt, Francis. *Healing.* New York: Bantam Books, 1974.

MacNutt, Francis. *The Power to Heal.* Notre Dame, IN: Ave Maria Press, 1977.

Miller, Patrick D. *They Cried to the Lord: The Form and Theology of Biblical Prayer.* Minneapolis: Fortress Press, 1994.

Occasional Services. Minneapolis: Augsburg Publishing House, 1982.

Olsen, Peder. *Healing through Prayer.* Minneapolis: Augsburg Publishing House, 1962.

Peterman, Mary E. *Healing: A Spiritual Adventure.* Philadelphia: Fortress Press, 1974.

Pfatteicher, Phillip H. *Commentary on the Occasional Services.* Philadelphia: Fortress Press, 1983.

Sanford, Agnes. *The Healing Light.* New York: Ballantine Books, 1983.

Sanford, Agnes. *The Healing Gifts of the Spirit.* New York: Jove Publishing, Inc., 1976.

Sanford, John A. *Healing and Wholeness.* Ramsey, NJ: Paulist Press, 1977.

Sanford, John A. *Kingdom Within: A Study of the Inner Meaning of Jesus' Sayings.* New York: Harper and Row, 1970.

Sharing: A Journal of Christian Healing. San Antonio, TX: The International Order of St. Luke the Physician.

Shleman, Barbara Leahy. *To Heal As Jesus Healed.* Notre Dame, IN: Ave Maria Press, 1978.

Guiding Children and Youth in Prayer

For Adults—About Children

Caplan, Theresa and Frank. *The Early Childhood Years: The Two to Six Year Old.* New York: The Putnam Publishing Group/Perigee, 1983.

Chapin, Alice. *Building Your Child's Faith.* Nashville: Thomas Nelson Publishers, 1990.

Droege, Thomas A. *Faith Passages and Patterns.* Philadelphia: Fortress Press, 1983.

Eyre, Linda and Richard. *Teaching Your Children Values.* New York: Simon and Schuster, 1993.

Fitzpatrick, Jean Grasso. *Something More.* New York: Viking Penguin, 1992.

Fowler, James W. *Stages of Faith: The Psychology of Human Development and the Quest for Meaning.* San Francisco: Harper San Francisco, 1981.

Juengst, Sara Coven. *Sharing Faith with Children.* Louisville: Westminster/John Knox Press, 1994.

Kohlberg, Lawrence and Lickona, Thomas. *The Stages of Ethical Development: From Childhood Through Old Age.* San Francisco: Harper San Francisco, 1986.

Wangerin, Walter Jr. *Little Lamb, Who Made Thee? A Book About Children and Parents.* Grand Rapids: Zondervan, 1993. (This book is also offered as *Little Lamb Audio Pages*.)

Westerhoff, John H. III. *Bringing Up Children in the Christian Faith.* San Francisco: Harper San Francisco, 1984.

Westerhoff, John H. III. *Will Our Children Have Faith?* San Francisco: Harper San Francisco, 1983.

For Families with Children of All Ages

Come to the Feast: Celebrating Lent, Holy Week, and Easter in the Home. Minneapolis: Augsburg Fortress, annual.

Horn, Geoffrey and Arthur Cavanaugh. *Bible Stories for Children.* New York: Macmillan, 1980.

O'Neal, Debbie Trafton. *An Easter People: Family Devotional Activities for Lent and Easter.* Minneapolis: Augsburg Fortress, 1990.

_____. *Before and After Christmas: Activities and Ideas for Advent and Epiphany.* Minneapolis: Augsburg Fortress, 1992.

_____. *Before and After Easter: Activities and Ideas for Lent to Pentecost.* Minneapolis: Augsburg Fortress, 1993.

Nappa, Mike and Amy. *52 Fun Family Devotions: Exploring and Discovering God's Word.* Minneapolis: Augsburg Fortress, 1994.

Proclaim the Word: Celebrating Summer, Autumn, and November in the Home. Minneapolis: Augsburg Fortress, annual.

Torvend, Samuel, ed. *Welcome Home: Scripture, Prayers, and Blessings for the Household (Year A).* Minneapolis: Augsburg Fortress, 1995.

Welcome the Light: Celebrating Advent, Christmas and Epiphany in the Home. Minneapolis: Augsburg Fortress, annual.

White, William R. *Speaking in Stories: Resources for Christian Storytellers.* Minneapolis: Augsburg Fortress, 1982.

Guiding Infants and Toddlers in Prayer

Carle, Eric. *The Very Busy Spider.* New York: The Putnam Publishing Group/Philomel, 1984.

Carle, Eric. *The Very Hungry Caterpillar.* New York: The Putnam Publishing Group/Philomel, 1981.

My First Prayer Series. Minneapolis: Augsburg Fortress, 1990.

My Little Bible Picture Book. Elgin, IL: David C. Cook, 1988.

O'Neal, Debbie Trafton. *Now I Lay Me Down to Sleep.* Minneapolis: Augsburg Fortress, 1994.

_____. *Thank You For This Food.* Minneapolis: Augsburg Fortress, 1994.

Guiding Preschoolers and Kindergartners in Prayer

Fitzgerald, Annie. *Dear God Books.* Minneapolis: Augsburg Fortress, 1984.

Fletcher, Sarah. *Prayers for Little People.* St. Louis: Concordia, 1974.

Marshall, Catherine. *Catherine Marshall's Story Bible.* New York: Avon, 1985.

O'Neal, Debbie Trafton. *My Read-and-Do Bible Storybook.* Minneapolis: Augsburg Fortress, 1989.

Simon, Mary Manz. *Little Visits on the Go: The Sing-Along and Share-a-Song Handbook.* St. Louis: Concordia, 1992.

Thomas, Mark. *The First Step Bible.* San Diego: Questar Publishing, 1994.

Guiding Lower Elementary Children in Prayer

Batchelor, Mary. *The Children's Bible in 365 Stories.* Elgin, IL: Lion Publishing, 1987.

de Paola, Tomie. *Tomie de Paola's Book of Bible Stories.* Grand Rapids: Zondervan, 1990.

Watson, Carol. *365 Children's Prayers.* Elgin, IL: Lion Publishing, 1989.

Yeatman, Linda. *A Child's Book of Prayers.* New York: Stewart, Tabori, & Chang, 1992.

Guiding Upper Elementary Children in Prayer

Augsburg Story Bible. Minneapolis: Augsburg Fortress, 1992.

Clare, John D. and Henry Wandsbrough. *The Bible Alive: Be a Witness to the Great Events of the Bible.* San Francisco: Harper San Francisco, 1993.

Egermeier, Elsie P. *Egermeier's Bible Story Book.* Anderson, IN: Warner Press, 1969.

Sorenson, Stephen W. *Growing Up Is an Adventure, Lord: Bible Devotions for Boys.* Minneapolis: Augsburg Fortress, 1992.

Wade, Evelyn Amuedo. *We're in This Together, Lord: Bible Devotions for Girls.* Minneapolis: Augsburg Fortress, 1992.

Guiding Middle School Teens in Prayer

Coleman, William L. *Entering the Teen Zone: Devotions to Guide You.* Minneapolis: Augsburg Fortress, 1991.

LeVander, Dyan. *Where Do I Fit In?: Prayers for Young Teens.* Minneapolis: Augsburg Fortress, 1989.

Weisheit, Eldon. *Psalms for Teens.* St. Louis: Concordia, 1992.

Guiding Senior High Teens in Prayer

Doud, Guy. *God Loves Me—So What?* St. Louis: Concordia, 1992.

On-line with God: Christians at Prayer — Outdoor Ministries Curriculum. Chicago: Evangelical Lutheran Church in America, 1995.

Swanson, Steve. *Faith Journeys: Youth Devotions by Nine Youth Writers.* Minneapolis: Augsburg Fortress, 1991.

_____ and 13 youth writers. *Faith Prints: Youth Devotions for Every Day of the Year.* Minneapolis: Augsburg Fortress, 1985.

NOTES

1. Theodore G. Tappert, trans. and ed., *The Book of Concord* (Philadelphia: Fortress Press, 1959), 213:16.

2. *Newsweek*, January 6, 1992, "Talking To God," p. 40.

3. *Life*, March 1994, "Why We Pray," pp. 54-63.

4. Walt Kallestad and Tim Schey, *Total Quality Ministry* ™ (Minneapolis: Augsburg Fortress, 1994), p. 48.

5. See C. Peter Wagner, *Prayer Shield: How to Intercede for Pastors, Christian Leaders, and Others on the Front Line* (Ventura, CA: Regal Books, 1992).

6. For more information, contact David Bryant, Concerts of Prayer International, 901 East 78th Street, Bloomington MN 55420.

Face to Face with God

Face to Face with God

Face to Face with God

Face to Face with God

Face to Face with God

Face to Face with God

Face to Face with God

Face to Face with God

Face to Face with God

Face to Face with God

January	January
February	February
March	March
April	April
May	May
June	June
July	July
August	August
September	September
October	October
November	November
December	December